A WOMAN'S GUIDE TO

INNER
CHILD
HEALING

A WOMAN'S GUIDE TO

INNER

CHILD

HEALING

Overcome Trauma, Recognize Your Feelings,
Learn to Let the Past Go, and
Become the Best Version of Yourself

GLORIA ZHANG, MA

Published by:
Ulysses Press
PO Box 3440
Berkeley, CA 94703
www.ulyssespress.com

ISBN: 978-1-64604-547-1
Library of Congress Control Number: 2023938328

Printed in the United States by Versa Press
10 9 8 7 6 5 4 3 2 1

Acquisitions editor: Claire Sielaff
Managing editor: Claire Chun
Editor: Renee Rutledge
Proofreader: Barbara Schultz
Front cover design: Rebecca Lown
Interior design: what!design @ whatweb.com
Layout: Winnie Liu

To my grandparents, with whom my safe place resides: *Wo ai ni.*

To Mom, Dad, and Adele: Through the trials and tribulations, we found love underneath. Because of you, I am the woman I am today.

To Andrew, you are my heart.

And, finally, to all of my listeners and students whom I learn from every single day: I love you all, besties.

CONTENTS

HOW TO USE THIS BOOK

Bestie, I see you.

You're here because you realize there's something deep inside you that wants to be witnessed — something that's begging to be healed.

You're here because you're stuck in a repetitive pattern in your life and can't seem to get out of it. You're not even sure why you keep getting into bad situations.

Maybe old childhood memories bubbled up to the surface by accident, and they've taken you by storm! Perhaps you've been blindsighted by a breakup, or maybe you googled the words "inner-child healing" and made your way to these pages.

Is it just bad luck? Is it brain chemistry? I don't think so.

A modern world where we're encouraged to suppress, numb, or medicate our symptoms beckons a deeper question: What is the *root cause* of our struggles? I believe the answer lies in our childhood experiences.

Whatever brought you to this book, I believe you were meant to find it. Welcome!

I wrote this book with you in mind. After noticing that other books on this topic can be a bit too intense for beginners, I designed this one to be a gentler guide for your journey. You've done such a brave thing in showing up today. It's going to be worth it!

What you'll need:
- A (sparkly) pen
- A notebook
- Your favorite tea
- The willingness to truly look within
- Optional: cozy blankets, pixie dust, and your favorite snacks

After I hit a million downloads on *The Inner Child Podcast*, a ton of people have asked me to write this book. Although the book took me a few months to write, it actually took many years of experience in working with clients to form the methods, ideas, and tools it contains.

Throughout *A Woman's Guide to Inner Child Healing*, you'll see journal exercises and activity prompts designed to take you deeper into the truth of where your current suffering actually comes from. My suggestion? *Do them.* Just as you couldn't learn how to drive a car just by staring at a driving manual (you'd need to get into the front seat and drive!), there are many concepts in this book that will only make sense when you put them into practice.

As a relationship coach and former psychotherapist, I've had tremendous success helping hundreds of women permanently break free of toxic relationships and find their life partners using my unique three-phase method. The additional benefits of this work have included healing generational trauma, friendships, financial blockages, and more. I present the three *Feel, Heal, Attract* pillars in a certain order for a reason, so trust the process and ignore the urge to skip ahead!

Doing the work of inner-child healing, without taking any shortcuts, will ultimately lead you back home to yourself, permanently out of your cycle of suffering.

The inner-child healing tools inside this book truly saved my life and have improved countless clients' lives. I've made it my life mission to help as many people as I can by sharing this knowledge.

The painful events that happened to you as a child were not your fault. But what happens *next* is your responsibility.

I hope you'll love the massive perspective shift you'll gain from this guide so that you, too, can discover the relief of healing your inner-child.

XOXO,

Gloria

Note: There are real success stories from women I've worked with that you'll see throughout this book. Client names and details have been changed for privacy purposes. Any accompanying resources and printables can be grabbed for free from my website at WomansGuideToInnerChildHealing.com.

INTRODUCTION

"Heal the girl, and the woman will appear."
—Unknown

Girl, what happened to the magic?

Remember the butterflies you felt as a child when seeing the mesmerizing stars in the sky? Or being that little girl with a big heart who wanted to befriend every cashier at the supermarket? Or belting out your favorite songs in public—without a care in the world?

As brand-new souls, we started off as the most vibrant expression of ourselves before the social conditioning, traumas, and hardships of the world took place.

But for some of you, this magic was cut short by tragic life circumstances. You might have lost your beloved mother or father to absence, alcoholism, or death. You might have been criticized, condemned, ignored, and deprived of love and attention. Some of you reading may have even been raised by cruel abusers and robbed of the opportunity for a safe and beautiful childhood.

For others, the hardship may not have been as obvious. Maybe you had a picture-perfect family and a roof over your head, yet behind closed doors, there was no warmth or emotional comfort. You might have struggled with reconciling this feeling that something was missing.

Or maybe your family wasn't picture perfect at all. You might have grown up feeling envious of your classmates with "normal" families, daydreaming of what it would feel like to have a "normal" Christmas or do "normal" kid things.

Some of you would watch movies at school about "big, happy families," then go home to cold and broken households. As years and decades passed, this may have hardened you into your adult shell. You may have continued to stumble through life searching for a glimpse of that magic again. Some of you may have sought affection in the arms of relationships and one-night stands. Or buried the pain in endless office work and anti-anxiety medications. Perhaps you occasionally found relief during an intoxicated karaoke night, for a brief moment of uninhibited freedom.

For myself, this drunken stupor occurred on a monthly basis!

"How the hell did this happen to me?" I would ponder of my half-awake, hungover state while dragging my reluctant body to a nine-to-five job. I thought, surely, life must have more meaning than dragging around my childhood traumas, chasing after the love that I didn't receive when I was young.

As a therapist myself, even I didn't have all the answers! Still, I searched for them on meditation retreats, ayahuasca ceremonies across Peru, and even six-week self-help programs. All of these tools would make me feel better for a few months, but eventually the floodgates would reopen and all of my negative patterns and self-sabotaging would be back. Have you ever felt this type of hopelessness?

It was pure accident that I stumbled upon the concept of inner-child work while desperately searching for a solution to my repetitive self-destructive patterns. When digging into some research on online forums, I got instant full-body chills when I read the insight that "grown-ups are just little kids walking around in adult bodies." Just like that, I heard the voice of Little Gloria for the first time in years. I had been running around the globe trying to "fix" my grown-up self when there was a lonely child within me who was begging for my attention. She was hurt. She was tired. But most of all, she needed me to finally stop running and take care of her.

Even more importantly, I finally understood that the reason my past healing felt like temporary solutions was because I wasn't penetrating deep enough to the root of the trauma. It wasn't enough to simply talk about the anxiety—I needed to find the origin of that anxiety.

From then on, I dedicated my life to deep diving into healing my inner girl, and my life took a 180-degree turn. Within months, I met the love of my life and entered my first healthy relationship. I also healed the root of my anxious and people-pleasing habits. I attracted and manifested many travel, speaking, and friendship opportunities at a speed that was unfathomable. And a few years ago, I launched *The Inner Child Podcast,* which quickly became one of the most downloaded healing podcasts on the internet. By using inner-child work, my clients were also healing at a faster time frame than ever, and the benefits continued months and years after we had worked together.

Not only was the magic back—it was here to stay! I can truly say that I feel more like a child now in my thirties than I did when I was an actual kid. I feel so alive and I believe that my life has just begun.

So girl, it's time for you to shine.

Let's help you get your magic back too.

CHAPTER 1

WHAT IS YOUR INNER-CHILD?

"The most sophisticated people I know — inside they are all children."
—Jim Henson

I know that the concept of the inner-child seems bizarre or even hokey at first, but let's suspend our disbeliefs for a moment. Isn't it weird that you can still remember what it was like being younger, as if it were yesterday? That's because your younger self is still you!

Your inner-child is a metaphor for your childlike essence. Carl Jung described the "divine child" as a symbol or archetype. The art therapist Lucia Capacchione was one of the first pioneers behind the idea of being able to "re-parent" your inner-child by becoming your own parent. Then, in the 1980s, a new branch of therapy was born called Internal Family Systems that helped people reconnect with the different parts within ourselves.

I stand on the shoulders of giants who paved the way to this incredible work. Today, I define your inner-child as the real, authentic aspect of you that captures your soul's essence. It's who you were before the traumas, societal conditioning, and complicated parents. And while I don't love using the word "pure," this word does capture the natural state that you were in as a child.

The inner-child is the young you that existed when you took your first breath in this life. It's the two-year-old version of you who used to stare wondrously at the season's first snowfall and skip over all the cracks on the sidewalk without a care. And though you are no longer a child in physical form, this aspect of yourself remains a part of you forever. Your shoe size just got a bit bigger!

Almost every adult problem you have now has its roots from way back when you were little.

In order to heal you as an adult, we need to heal the child inside you first. And that first step comes with figuring out who your inner-child is!

However, don't make the mistake of believing your inner-child is a perfect angel! This is often a story we project onto the innocence of kids. In reality, your inner-child is multidimensional and complicated and damn well deserves to be loved for all of it. Yes, they are creative, spontaneous, and pure joy. However, they are also mischievous, curious, silly, and chaotic. The catch is that your inner-child desires to be accepted for *all* of these parts, not just the parts that we deem to be acceptable by society's standards.

JOURNAL PROMPTS

1. What comes to mind when you think of the words "inner-child"? Do these words strike a chord? Do they come across as cheesy or uncomfortable? Why?

2. How connected or disconnected do you feel with your inner-child? Is it easy to connect with the younger part of yourself just by thinking about it? Or does your relationship with your younger self feel detached?

3. Considering that we have many layers to our personalities, what traits and characteristics come up for you when you think of your inner-child? Allow yourself to observe the complexity of your inner-child and celebrate it! They may be sweet and friendly but also enjoy playing pranks and breaking rules!

4. Have you honored all of the parts of you? Do you judge certain characteristics as "bad" or "good"? Where did you pick up these messages? How can you be more accepting of all of your parts?

CHAPTER 2

HOW TO CONNECT WITH LITTLE YOU

Getting in touch with your inner-child is sort of like a reunion with a distant cousin you haven't seen in ten years. It's awkward and uncomfortable, yet you both secretly hope the other one breaks the ice! Just like any relationship, the one with your inner-child is going to take time and patience to rebuild. This is especially true if you have neglected your own needs for a long time. Your inner-child may even feel as if they cannot trust you, and you will need more time to gain the trust back.

TIP #1: FIND A PHOTO OF LITTLE YOU

The simplest place to start is to find a photo of yourself when you were young and stick it somewhere visible for the duration of working through this handbook. Choose a photo that you feel most drawn toward. If you do not have any photos of yourself, skip to Tip #2.

Take a deep breath and remember that whatever comes up for you is normal. Sometimes we see our inner-child in a carefree state, and other times we see them in pain or in settings associated with bad memories. It can be distressing to associate this part of ourselves with difficult scenarios, so take breaks when sorting through old photo albums and get support as needed.

PASTE YOUR PHOTO HERE!

TIP #2: DRAW A PICTURE OF LITTLE YOU

Art can paint a more emotional picture of your inner-child. What comes to mind when you think of the words "inner-child"? If you connect with the younger part of you, how would you draw them? What shapes, colors, and textures come through? Some people express their inner-child through drawings of animals, flowers, or scribbles.

If you find it difficult to draw, remember that art is simply an expression and isn't supposed to look perfect! As long as your true feelings are conveyed, then you've done the exercise right.

DRAW YOUR INNER CHILD!

JOURNAL PROMPTS

1. In what environment do you envision your inner-child? Examples: In a field of flowers, trapped inside a box, hiding under the bed, etc.

_____

2. What emotions do you feel when you look at the picture you have drawn of your inner-child? For example, does your picture fill you with joy, nostalgia, or love? Or does it activate feelings of sadness, anger, or grief? Remember that there is no right or wrong answer! Your reaction simply illuminates what needs to be healed.

_____

3. How does your inner-child seem to feel about you? If your inner-child could talk to you, what would they say? Does there seem to be a disconnect? Do they seem to be happy to see you, or are they upset?

_____
_____
_____
_____

TIP #3: THINK BACK TO A CHILDHOOD MEMORY

Think back to a childhood memory in which you were safe, you were connected, or you experienced a little moment of joy.

Even if you feel you do not have many happy memories, most people have tiny instances of fun or joyful moments sprinkled throughout childhood. In fact, a very bizarre thing happened to me a few years ago when rewatching old family tapes. I had always recalled my early years with a lot of pain and grief. It was as if a dark gloomy Instagram filter had been applied to my entire childhood. But, to my surprise, there were hours of home video footage of eight-year-old me spinning around and belting out Whitney Houston songs at the top of my lungs! Indeed, trauma can cause certain memories to be "forgotten," repressed, or buried away in the mind.

So, consider using cues to remind you of moments of joy that you did experience. Did you have a favorite toy? A favorite candy bar? A special "place"? Who were the (perhaps rare) safe and loving people in your life?

I recall a conversation with a previous client in my Situationship to Soulmate program, which is a program I developed to help women attract healthy love by recovering from toxic relationships that go nowhere (which I refer to as **situationships**). This client swore up and down that they had absolutely no positive memories at all. Then, around the holidays, they recalled the one safe person in their life—their grandmother. Each Christmas, they would leave an abusive household and spend the holidays with their dearly beloved grandma for a day. What might be considered just a fun day for other kids was this client's saving grace that gave them the strength to go on. My client had forgotten about these memories until recently, and they teared up when recalling Grandma's noodle soup and sing-song voice.

JOURNAL PROMPTS

Try connecting all five senses (sight, smell, hearing, taste, touch) to a happy or neutral memory from when you were a child.

1. Buy your favorite childhood snack. Write about how you felt as you ate it then, and how you feel as you eat it now. For example, was there a candy bar that all the kids liked to eat in school? Does it still bring you joy to taste it now?

2. Find a nice smell that links back to a childhood memory. Write down a description of that smell. Examples: Grandmother's famous gumbo soup or the comforting scent of your favorite teacher's cologne.

3. Think of a vision, such as that of an object or place, that reminds you of a pleasant memory. Write down the name of the object and the associated memory. For example, a red balloon can bring up a sharp memory of a happy day out with your mother. The beautiful mountains can remind you of visiting your relatives.

4. Recall a sound that reminds you of a pleasant memory. Write it down. Examples: Someone singing you a special lullaby to put you to sleep. Your favorite song that played on the radio.

5. Physically pick up or touch precious objects from your childhood. Write what they are. Examples: A special blanket, a stuffed toy, a rock.

TIP #4: TAPPING INTO TV SHOWS OR MOVIES

Something about music has the power to tap into different parts of us. As a proud "Disnerd," I instantly revert back to a giddy toddler anytime I hear the opening of *The Little Mermaid*. I also get a flood of adrenaline whenever I catch a riff of the Backstreet Boys or Spice Girls!

1. What #throwback songs help you connect to a younger you?

_____

_____

_____

_____

_____

2. Here are some helpful questions to ask yourself: Think about movies or shows that left an impact on you as a child, or that you watched on repeat. What music was popular at the time when you were a kid?

_____

_____

_____

_____

_____

3. Were there any specific songs that you loved?

_____

_____

_____

_____

_____

JOURNAL PROMPTS

1. Go on YouTube and search for your favorite childhood songs or television theme music. Write down how you feel in your body when you hear them.

2. Try singing your old favorite songs out loud. Reflect on how the lyrics make you feel.

3. Do any memories come up when you reexperience this media?

TIP #5: TALK IN A BABY VOICE TO YOURSELF!

While this might sound like a weird suggestion (and one that may get you some odd looks depending on who's around you!), inner-child healing using a baby voice can also be a lot of fun! But if you think about it, people naturally revert to a baby voice when they feel the most safe. They do this with intimate partners, their pets, and sometimes after a glass of wine!

Speaking in a baby voice seems to feel very comforting for a lot of people. It almost seems to activate body memories inside the throat and is one tool that you can add to your toolkit.

Ideas for when to use a baby voice:

- When comforting yourself during tough times
- When talking to your pet
- When answering these journal questions out loud

CHAPTER 3

HOW TO COMMUNICATE WITH YOUR INNER-CHILD

So, how do you communicate with your inner-child?

You talk to them, duh!

The easiest way to make a connection with your inner-child is to strike up a conversation! Coming up with questions can be tricky, so here is a list of suggestions. See if you can hear or feel an answer arise when asking them.

1. Hey, it's me! Do you remember me?
2. How are you feeling?
3. What did you do today?
4. How can I help you today?
5. Do you want anything from me?

Some folks are met with an overjoyed child who is running over, ecstatic to see them! For others, the inner-child is avoidant, silent, and anxiously hiding in the corner. As the parent to your own inner kid, you have the opportunity to respond to them the right way this time. Be as patient, loving, and kind as you would be with a real child!

Here are some ideas of things to say to help build trust:
• I've found you now, and I'm never leaving you alone again.
• I have missed you.
• I commit to earning your trust that I will always stay.
• I'm going to put you first from now on.
• I can handle *all* your feelings, big or small.
• I am learning how to keep you safe from harm.
• I am so proud of you.
• I am committing to paying attention to your needs, big or small.
• I am not perfect, but I'll always say sorry when I'm in the wrong.

Did you feel something inside you from reading this?

Sometimes connecting with your inner-child makes you want to burst into tears or scream. This is normal.

Let yourself cry. Hold yourself, gently rocking back and forth, until you feel safe and sound again. There's nothing to worry about now. You are home.

Spend about once a day checking in with this part of yourself, and you will surely witness the start of a beautiful relationship.

WHAT DOES YOUR INNER GIRL WANT TO BE CALLED?

Maybe it's a nickname. Or they might respond well to a term of endearment. Take a look at the examples below and give them a try:

- Darling
- Dear
- Little one
- My love
- Cupcake

- Muffin
- Sweetheart
- My heart
- Precious
- Special one

JOURNAL PROMPTS

1. How did adults typically treat your inner-child? Did they actually listen to you? Did they take your thoughts and emotions seriously? Were they patient and loving?

_____

_____

_____

_____

_____

2. Are you repeating any old patterns by the way you're approaching your inner-child? Are you becoming impatient and pushing your inner-child the same way that the other adults did? Are you judging and misunderstanding them? Are you being critical of them?

_____

_____

_____

_____

_____

3. How does your inner-child *need* to be approached? Do they want to open up when they're ready? Are they scared of being bombarded by so many questions? Do they want a fun conversation first? Do they need hugs instead of words? Do they want to draw instead?

_____

_____

_____

_____

_____

4. What do you need to do to start building trust with your inner-child again? Do you need to allow them to open up on their own time? Do you need to reassure them that you are here to help, not hurt? Do you need to use a gentler voice?

_____

_____

_____

_____

_____

CHAPTER 4

WHY DOES BAD SH** KEEP HAPPENING TO ME?

"People raised on love see things differently than those raised on survival."
—Joy Marino

THE ORIGINAL WOUND

Ever wonder why life feels like a broken record sometimes? Why do we keep running back to the same things that cause us pain, even when we know it's bad for us?!

Easy answer: because we have wounds.

Our original "wound" started long, long ago.

You became a baby soul after being separated from the Universe, God, Higher Self, The Great Spirit, Source, or whichever word you align with the most. Atoms from stars that have been around for billions of years began to form your body. Out of the darkness, your first attachment began: Mother's nurturing umbilical cord. At seven weeks, you started to sprout arms and legs. By 24 weeks, your organs were fully formed. Encased by the comforting, familiar beating of Mom's heart, there's never a moment that you were alone.

Then, your human life began when you were ripped away from your mother's womb in a traumatic event called birth. Your first gasping breath took place after drowning in your own lung's fluids. Loud frightening sounds and scary images overwhelmed the five senses in your little vulnerable body. It's utterly disorienting! You'd go on to spend your entire life searching for what make you feel whole again.

As a separated lone creature, you helplessly depended on your parents or caregivers to help you get on your feet. If you were lucky, you were filled with enough love and care to offset that original wound of separation, and you would have realized the truth that you're already whole and complete. Just like a tiny leaf is a perfect aspect of the whole tree, you are already a perfect singular expression of the Universe. You would have understood that you *are* enough, and being enough means you feel safe to give and love freely. This would have given you the courage to survive all of the additional separations that life forces upon us: moving out, breakups, economic recessions, deaths. You would have been able to deal with life a lot better.

But if you didn't receive adequate nurturing and support, then you didn't feel like you were enough. You may have felt abandoned, ignored, neglected, hurt by your parents (who were also wounded and imperfect humans, sadly enough). That original wound of separation grew into a more global wound of feeling incomplete and broken. You resisted and broke down after each life challenge. Each additional separation felt like breaking off more pieces of you. These childhood wounds are what I call "Core Wounds."

You may have tried searching for wholeness in relationships, in sex, in climbing the corporate ladder, in self-medication, or in chasing material things and status. But it never felt enough, did it? You would momentarily escape into the rush of excitement, only to come tumbling back down to how you've always felt. By doing this work, you'll realize that nothing outside of you can make you feel whole that isn't already within yourself.

However, there is hope! What I've found is that when you learn how to re-parent yourself to learn this truth, then you can become free of this cycle. You can feel good without depending on external quick fixes. You can live in a state of authentic joy and magic. And when we break our own cycles of pain, we make the world a better place for our descendants and fellow beings.

THE FOUR CORE WOUNDS
FROM CHILDHOOD

"My life's dream is to dance off into the forest, and [lie] naked eating M&M's."

Although this isn't the revelation you might expect from the boss-babe of a big engineering company, these were their words during our biggest breakthrough session yet.

Like many of my clients, Emily had a rough start to life in a prisonlike childhood with a tyrannical, alcoholic mother. From that, this little suburban girl grew into a tough woman who spearheaded their way to the top of a male-dominated industry. Thirty years of cutthroat hustling and eventual complete burnout, all to prove that they would never again allow Mom (or anyone) to control them.

Emily was a badass, and I adored working with them! And as planned, nobody ever controlled adult Emily. In fact, nobody could even come *close* to them and the walls they had built around their heart. But even with these impenetrable walls, adult life was not all smooth sailing. Emily had two children of their own and even went through a messy divorce. And beneath all of that, Little Emily was longing for the freedom to be their true, wild, childlike self. But it seemed impossible. Emily could still hear their mother's yells, could still feel their mother's disappointment.

The irony is that by the time clients slide into my DMs, their problematic parents are usually out of the picture or dead. So then why do they continue living haunted by the ghosts of abusive, neglectful, or immature parents?

After a decade of working with high-performers who come from difficult childhoods, I can only sum things up in one sentence: We simply gravitate toward what's familiar to us, even when we know it's bad for us! It's because you are unconsciously re-creating the same unresolved traumas and wounds from childhood well into your adulthood.

For example, if your dad abandoned you as a child, you may find yourself in the same types of relationships with emotionally unavailable men. You may even feel highly triggered by a boss who embodies similar qualities. Despite vowing never to be rejected again, your body is still attracted to the familiarity of men who remind you of your flaky father. That darn Freud is rolling in his grave as we speak!

Why does this happen though? It's very simple. It's because familiar feels comfortable to us, even when it's not safe. The brain would rather experience predictable chaos than uncertain peace. Sure, it may end up in more trauma, but at least we know exactly what to expect. Plus the thrilling highs and lows of dysfunctional situations can intoxicate us into staying in something a lot longer than we want to admit.

If we go one level deeper, we can see that your inner-child may also be attempting to resolve an old wound by conquering this new situation. On a subconscious level this can look like, "If I can impress this *new* person enough to stay with me, maybe it will make up for daddy leaving me."

If we go another layer deeper, we then touch that original wound from birth. It's that deep, existential anxiety of living as separated, isolated beings. It's only through connection that we find safety with each other, but only if we've healed enough within ourselves to have the capacity to maintain healthy relationships.

Girl, I promise it's not you. It's actually about what happened to you a long time ago.

Most of us have some, or all, of the four **Core Wounds** from childhood. In addition to the original existential wound, Core Wounds are the additional wounds that occur in your childhood that form the root of your adult problems. This splitting can happen when your caregiver failed to meet your needs as a child, and those needs can resurface in adulthood just as untreated wounds can reopen and cause more pain.

It doesn't matter how old you are, or where you're from. It's possible to address these wounds so that your patterns no longer need to repeat through life!

I must warn you that discovering your Core Wounds can be absolutely life-changing. You will start to see that your whole life has been a pattern unfolding beyond your awareness. When I discovered my abandonment wound, I realized that it controlled every aspect of my life, from choosing to date men who would always leave me, to my chronic habit of overworking out of the irrational fear of being fired, to even the tiniest quirks like oversmiling so that waitresses would like me and not "abandon" my order!

So, what are the Core Wounds and which Core Wounds do you have? Take this quick quiz and check the statements that apply to you. If you check five or more sentences in each category, it suggests you may have wounding under that criteria. Please note that this quiz is just a general guideline and not a standardized tool.

THE ABANDONMENT WOUND

- ○ You fear being abandoned or rejected.
- ○ You believe that people always end up leaving you.
- ○ You fear being unlovable.
- ○ You people-please to win others' approval.
- ○ You often feel like an outsider, even around familiar people.
- ○ You hold onto unhealthy relationships longer than you should.
- ○ You abruptly end relationships to avoid getting hurt.
- ○ You may feel attracted to or obsessed with people who are aloof or emotionally unavailable.
- ○ You may have experienced abandonment on a systemic level, such as racism, sexism, ableism, homophobia, etc.

THE TRUST WOUND

- ○ You have a hard time trusting other people.
- ○ You experienced a serious unexpected loss (like death, injury, illness, divorce).
- ○ You have a hard time trusting that "good things can happen."
- ○ You believe that everyone will always ends up hurting you or letting you down.
- ○ You are afraid of being "too happy" out of fear of losing it.
- ○ You are afraid of loved ones dying or becoming injured.
- ○ You don't allow yourself to depend on others.
- ○ You don't get too close to people.

- ○ You avoid giving people the opportunity to let you down.
- ○ You are quick to assume the worst in others.
- ○ You may "hurt others before they hurt you."
- ○ Ironically, you may also end up with the wrong people due to familiarity.
- ○ You may have experienced trust issues on a systemic level, such as racism, sexism, ableism, homophobia, etc.

THE GUILT WOUND

- ○ You are an empath who easily feels others' emotions.
- ○ You feel burdened by taking responsibility for others' feelings.
- ○ You have survivor's guilt after someone else dies or suffers.
- ○ You try to anticipate people's needs before they tell you.
- ○ You have difficulty setting boundaries.
- ○ You feel guilty or ashamed easily.
- ○ You feel gullible or easily taken advantage of.
- ○ You never feel like you're doing enough.
- ○ You feel resentful for agreeing to things you don't want.
- ○ You deny your own wants and needs to make others feel better.
- ○ You have a poorly developed sense of self and often don't know what you really want.
- ○ You burn out easily from doing too much.
- ○ You may have experienced guilt or boundary issues on a systemic level, such as racism, sexism, ableism, homophobia, etc.

THE NEGLECT WOUND

- ○ You often feel unseen, unappreciated, and ignored.
- ○ You feel like the black sheep or misfit who doesn't belong.
- ○ You tend to focus on how you are different from others rather than what you have in common.
- ○ In social situations, you automatically expect to become forgotten or ignored.
- ○ You feel like you're not special.
- ○ You don't feel like you're good enough.
- ○ You believe that you can only depend on yourself.
- ○ You struggle with letting grudges go.

○ You may neglect or procrastinate on taking care of your own needs and sometimes go days without eating properly or sleeping on time.
○ You struggle with putting yourself first.
○ You may have experienced exclusion on a systemic level, such as racism, sexism, ableism, homophobia, etc.

To learn more about the four Core Wounds, check out episode one of *The Inner Child Podcast*.

JOURNAL PROMPTS

1. In what situations do I feel abandoned by others? How do I normally deal with this?

2. In what situations do I have a hard time trusting other people? In what situations do I have a hard time trusting that good things happen? How do I normally deal with this?

3. In what situations do I take on too much guilt or responsibility? How do I normally deal with this?

4. In what situations do I feel ignored or neglected by others? How do I normally deal with this?

5. Which is my main Core Wound?

6. Do I have multiple Core Wounds? If so, how does this complexity impact me?

HOW DID I BECOME THIS WAY?

Now that you know what your Core Wounds are, let's delve into where they come from.

Pull out a journal, think back to your childhood, and see what answers spontaneously arise to these two important questions:

1. Whose love and approval did you crave the most growing up?

2. Who did you have to be, to deserve and win that love? What did this teach you?

Example:

1. Whose love and approval did you crave the most growing up?

As a child, I always longed for Mom's attention as they were the distant and emotionally unpredictable one. I feared them and was anxious whenever they were around, but at the same time also wanted their praise. I feel the most triggered around them.

2. Who did you have to be, to deserve and win that love? What did this teach you?

The only times Mom was nurturing to me was when I got sick, which I think taught me to learn that I need to become helpless in order to get attention. Other times, they would only pay attention to me when I did something great at school. This explains why I always put so much pressure on myself to study hard.

It's normal for these questions to bring tears if the feelings they bring up are of not being "good enough." Just remember that children don't have the knowledge and experience to regulate their emotions and understand what's going on. And even if your parents were doing their best, it's okay to acknowledge that their best still didn't meet your needs.

THE FOUR CORE WOUNDS

If you felt rejected by your parents, witnessed a messy divorce, or had to prove your worth to deserve their attention, you may have developed an **abandonment wound** that continues into your adulthood now. Many folks who were adopted or had parents who were rarely home can also develop an abandonment wound.

If your family lied, broke promises, or abused you, then naturally you would have developed a **trust wound**. This also seems to happen when kids learn about a parent's infidelity. In general, whenever a child learns that they cannot trust mom or dad it can end up manifesting into a pain point in the future.

A **guilt wound** can start even when a parent innocently sighs, "Oh baby, you're making mommy hurt their back." A child will truly believe that they are the cause of things around them. So if your parents blamed you for their own emotions, it taught you to believe that you are responsible for managing other people's behaviors and feelings. The guilt can also come from the fear of realizing that your parents can't regulate or help themselves, and the expectation to "grow up quickly" and take care of things falls on your shoulders. Many people with a guilt wound develop a coping mechanism of behaving like a caretaker or giver identity, and sometimes even role-reverse with their parents.

Finally, a **neglect wound** will grow if your physical or emotional needs weren't understood and met as a child. Everyone's experiences are different, and this can range from severe intentional neglect to the neglect of an immature parent who didn't understand that you needed hugs rather than words. Since as children we don't have the language to communicate or understand our own needs, we rely entirely on our parents to interpret and provide for us.

The bottom line is that your reactions when you were a child weren't your fault. I say this over and over again so that it really sinks in. You were just a kid. You were still growing in your limbs and body parts. You literally just arrived here yourself, so how was it fair to expect you to be anything other than a child?

WORKSHEET FOR THE CORE WOUNDS

THE ABANDONMENT WOUND

My inner-child believes that I have to be/do _____,
otherwise people will leave me.

The earliest time I remember feeling this way was _____.

The person who originally made me feel this way is _____.

Affirmation for abandonment wounds:

"Little one, I am learning how to make you the most important thing to me. You have nothing to prove. As your grown-up self, I will be here with you forever. You matter."

THE GUILT WOUND

My inner-child believes that I am responsible for _____,
and if I stop feeling guilty it means that I am _____.

The earliest time I remember feeling this way was _____.

The person who originally made me feel this way is _____.

Affirmation for guilt wounds:

"Darling, you are not responsible for others' reactions and behavior. It's safe to shine your light as brightly as you can. As your grown-up self, I can handle all your feelings, big or small."

THE NEGLECT WOUND

My inner-child believes that if I am _____,
then I will be forgotten and ignored.

The earliest time I remember feeling this way was _____.

The person who originally made me feel this way is _____.

Affirmation for neglect wounds:

"My love, I am learning to pay attention to all your needs, big or small. As your grown-up self, I will put you first no matter what. You are allowed to speak, play, and enjoy life freely."

THE TRUST WOUND

My inner-child believes that people will always hurt or betray me if I _____.

The earliest time I remember feeling this way was _____.

The person who originally made me feel this way is _____.

Affirmation for trust wounds:

"Little one, you deserve the world. You deserve love and kindness. As your grown-up self, I will be patient and earn your trust by respecting and listening to your needs. You are safe with me for the rest of our life."

CHAPTER 5

WHAT IF MY CHILDHOOD "WASN'T THAT BAD"?

"I had food on the table, a roof over my head, and every toy and pet I ever wanted. Nobody ever laid a hand on me. Then why, oh why, do I feel such seething resentment toward my parents?"

—Anonymous

I have had several clients over the years who check off every symptom on the list. They struggle with anxiety, with relationships, and feeling safe. But on paper, they appear to have had a very normal and stable life as a kid.

These clients compare themselves to others with "obvious" trauma (such as a car accident, or sexual abuse) and minimize their own experiences, meanwhile developing guilt about how they feel toward their parents. They begin questioning their own symptoms and wonder if they're overreacting. After all, they say, their parents weren't "that bad!"

If you fall in this category, I want to send you the biggest hug ever! You are not alone. I want to remind you that trauma is not a competition, where one form is pitted against the other.

I'm also aware of critics who worry that applying a trauma lens to life might be pathologizing "normal life" and putting thoughts into people's head. I understand why people have these concerns, and perhaps we can find a middle ground. First, as humans evolved through history, many things that used to be considered normal in the past are not seen as acceptable anymore (for example, owning a slave, or women being banned from voting). Secondly, if inner-child healing improves your well-being then that is proof enough your childhood had some impact on you. Isn't that the whole point, to improve people's lives?

I argue that at times, emotional needs are more important than physical needs. It becomes a lot easier to navigate an impending food shortage when there's love in the family and someone to lean on for support. But if your relationships are hollow and cold, suddenly it doesn't matter how many loaves of bread you have.

Emotional needs can include:

- Hugs, kisses, physical touch
- Hearing the words "I love you"
- Being listened to without distraction
- Uninterrupted play time together
- Feeling special, cherished, and loved
- Receiving praise and affection
- Receiving full, *real* smiles
- Having an adult name and validate your feelings
- Learning how to cope with your emotions through healthy examples or coaching
- Remembering your preferences, dreams, and goals

However, it doesn't count if your parent spent lots of time with you, but they were glued to their phone instead of interacting with you. Same thing if you only heard the words "I love you" when you got A's in school, but received the cold shoulder when you got C's.

Do you see why it's more difficult to pinpoint emotional needs versus physical needs? Because they are hard to point out, they can easily be dismissed as unimportant. But this couldn't be further from the truth.

One of my best, most cherished memories was spending a Christmas Eve with my family at a soup kitchen. It was a snowy night in Toronto. At the time, I had no idea that we needed free food in order to save up for my new winter boots. I didn't even know how embarrassed my parents felt while arriving at the church's doorsteps, lit up with warm holiday lights. When the doors opened, it was like walking into a new dimension. It didn't matter to me that we weren't at some fancy, five-star restaurant. But it did matter to me that I got to spend this entire holiday adventuring at this church with my special people.

> *"Trauma is not what happens to you. Trauma is what happens inside you as a result of what happens to you."*
>
> —Dr. Gabor Maté

Trauma is not a cookie-cutter experience. It's possible that losing a job will be perceived and experienced differently by different people. If you have a sensitive nervous system or poor self-esteem, you might be more impacted by certain events than others.

When obvious and major, one-time distressing events happen in our life, they are considered acute trauma. On the other hand, a series of multiple distressing experiences is called chronic, or complex trauma. For folks who have difficulty identifying specific traumatic events but rather endured a pattern of a *lack* of love, I describe this as "death by a thousand papercuts."

And if you prefer to get beyond the lens of trauma (after all, it is just one lens), it's helpful just to look at your upbringing in terms of needs. You had emotional and physical needs, and for whatever reasons, they didn't get met enough. Sometimes your parents did their best at the time, but it still wasn't enough because life is imperfect. For other folks, the intention was more cruel and malicious.

I had one such client who grew up in your typical suburban, middle-class family that went to all their soccer games and went out for ice cream every Sunday. Everything seemed fine, except for one important thing: Nobody was allowed to look sad or say "negative things" so that they could avoid making Mom feel upset. Like, ever. Anything remotely sad would make Mom really uncomfortable. Mom liked it best when everyone smiled. This meant that all conversations about disagreements, school bullying, or negative emotions were either ignored or swept under the rug. Nobody raised their voices or their hands. Nobody started confrontations.

On this surface this looked like one big, happy, cheerful family. But the child who was raised in that environment grew up to be a woman who couldn't identify or advocate for their own needs; they bottled up their own feelings, and had panic attacks when faced with any conflict in the real world. So the unmet needs for this woman were actually what *didn't* happen: the emotional safety and unconditional love from their mother.

Similarly, I experienced death by a thousand papercuts with my own father in the early stages of my childhood. He and my mom were a painfully hardworking couple who had moved here from China in search of a better life. I recall the guilt I experienced as I watched my dad devoting his entire existence to supporting me and my sister. It was traditional in my family's culture for parents to hide their affection physically. I often saw his hunched back leaving home at early hours, preparing for another long day at work. The consequence was that my father rarely had energy or patience by the time he arrived home. Instead of hugs and cuddles, I was met with a stone-cold face and curt replies. He never intended to hurt me, yet due to the circumstances that's just how things played out. How confusing it was to feel guilty for the sacrifice of his body for my basic needs, but also the yearning of my little heart for his love!

Remember that two things can exist at the same time. You can feel empathy for your parents while also validating that their actions hurt you. Humans can feel conflicting emotions all at the same time.

So, if you're still confused about your experience, here are three journaling questions to help validate your feelings:

JOURNAL PROMPTS

1. Despite things looking normal on the surface, was there a feeling that something was still missing? For example, maybe you had a roof over your head, but you didn't feel warm or safe to open up to your family. Your parents were wealthy business people, but you spent most of your time with a nanny. Your mother was present and engaged, but they frequently sounded annoyed or stressed. Your father always attended your school plays but was busy impressing other parents instead of celebrating you.

2. Did you feel like you could go to your caregivers about anything? Why or why not? When you were upset, were your caregivers the first people you would go to? Was there an unspoken rule that certain topics were off-limits? Did they ask you about how you felt?

3. What would happen if you allowed yourself to feel multiple emotions about your childhood at the same time? If you have mixed feelings about your childhood, it's okay for those feelings to coexist. For example, you can feel grateful that your immigrant parents wanted to give you a better life but also feel angry that they spent more time at work than with you.

SUBTLE WAYS YOU
ACTUALLY GOT HURT

Sometimes, it's just not obvious when our parents overlook our needs. It can make us question ourselves and wonder if it's all in our head. This is especially true when the source of our pain is the absence of loving actions, rather than something that actually happened. And trust me, the sense of having an unmet need is not in your head. Start with believing that there's always a reason behind each emotion. The checklist below is loosely based off the AMBIANCE system developed by Dr. Elisa Bronfman and Dr. Karlen Lyons-Ruth, which is a gold-standard measure used to assess how caregiver behaviors impact children (Bronfman, et al., 1992; Lyons-Ruth, et al., 1999). Go through this checklist and see if there are any subtle areas where you didn't get your needs met.

Note: The purpose of this exercise is not to imply that parents must be perfect in order to raise a healthy child! No human being can meet this expectation. Rather, this checklist is meant for you to identify which needs actually went unmet in your childhood. Our bodies communicate subtle body language that can make people feel safe or unsafe, even unconsciously. Children are highly sensitive to these cues!

SECURE PARENTING BEHAVIORS

- Offers expressive "real" smiles (genuine smiles that reach the eyes)
- Soothes child correctly when stressed; is comforting
- Reads cues when child wants to be picked up
- Intervenes when child engages in dangerous behavior, such as climbing a chair
- Mirrors facial expressions with body language
- Holds eye contact and is responsive
- Exudes a feeling of warmth
- Has a warm, calm, and soothing tone of voice

AVOIDANT CAREGIVER BEHAVIORS

- Has a frowning, angry, or "flat" face; avoids eye contact
- Doesn't pick up child or read cues for soothing, puts child down too soon, or ignores when child engages in dangerous behavior
- May initiate hugs but is the first to pull away
- Speaks in short, abrupt, loud, emotionless, or sarcastic tone of voice
- Is unenthusiastic or distracted during playtime (is on phone, doing work)
- Criticizes or minimizes child's feelings; lacks warmth
- Lacks facial mirroring

- Lacks body language mirroring
- Personalizes child's behavior ("Why are you doing that to me?")

ANXIOUS CAREGIVER BEHAVIORS

- Consistently shows a worried face, cries or displays pain in front of the child, or tries to make child feel guilty
- Has a lack of boundaries
- Disapproves of or punishes child for wanting space by withholding affection, being rude, etc.
- Is too careful, doesn't allow child to take risks
- Prioritizes their own needs instead of child's
- Relies on child as source of love and attention
- Takes child's behavior very personally ("Why do you hate me?")

DISORGANIZED CAREGIVER BEHAVIORS

- Shows discomfort of child (withdraws suddenly when child approaches, displays hesitancy in showing physical contact, tries to redirect child to toys instead)
- Indulges long silences, backs away, or holds object between themselves and child to create distance
- Puts child down too quickly, not fully soothing them
- Makes sharp, sudden movements that may scare child
- Makes an abrupt change in emotional display (sudden blank expression on face)
- Uses body language that leans away from child during interactions
- Gives conflicting messages; asks child to do something, then tells them not to do it
- Laughs or smiles when child cries or is upset

DID MY PARENTS HAVE TO BE PERFECT?

Not at all. When a child cries, a parent needs to determine what this behavior means. Is the child hungry? Scared? Tired? In need of a hug? Does this child even respond well to hugs? Parents who are emotionally in tune (or *attuned*) with their child can become present and engaged and may have a better likelihood of "guessing correctly." But even then, parents aren't going to get it right all the time.

In fact, a study done by Edward Tronick and Andrew Gianino showed that even in secure baby-parent relationships, the parent is only attuned about 30 percent of the time. This means that parents only need to "get it right" about a third of the time in order for a child to develop a secure relationship. In parenting language, this research is consistent with a concept called "good enough parenting" (Tronick and Gianino, 1986).

JOURNAL PROMPTS

1. Did anything surprise you as you went through the *Subtle Ways You Actually Got Hurt* list? How did this change the way you thought about your childhood?

2. Did you feel validated or relieved by seeing some of these items on the list?

3. In what ways can you forgive yourself for feeling resentful toward your parents?

CHAPTER 6

THE FEEL, HEAL, ATTRACT SYSTEM FOR RECOVERY

"Gloria, healing is so big and complicated. Do I meditate? Go to yoga? Journal twice a day? Breathe? Where do I even start?"

This is something I've heard from my clients time and time again. In the booming industry of self-help overwhelm and bajillions of Instagram posts, the problem isn't a lack of education. It's that there's *too much* information, so much so that you don't know where to start.

But as a high-achiever, I've always been an eager problem-solver for my clients. What's the point in my client spending three years getting a meditation certificate if at the end of the day, they still freeze up every time there's conflict in a relationship?

Or what about my other client who spent 15 years sitting in therapy but still can't understand why every guy they date turns out to be a narcissist?

Repeat after me: not *all* healing tools are made equal. And I don't believe meditation and affirmations are for everybody, nor are they necessary to heal. These tools are more like bells and whistles that can assist the healing journey.

A healing system needs to change the root of the wound and produce *real-world* benefits.

When it comes to recovering from trauma, the most widely accepted theory is the "3 Stages of Recovery," as described in Judith Herman's *Trauma and Recovery*. Judith describes the three stages as: safety and stabilization, remembrance and mourning, and reconnection and integration.

But in order to translate theory into results, I created the Feel, Heal, Attract System™ which has been tweaked and perfected over several years of my career with hundreds of clients. This system targets three specific areas for people to focus on in order to experience results:

1. FEEL: Find an easy way to process and regulate emotions so that you stop blindly reacting to your own overwhelming emotions. (See "What Are Your Eruptive Emotions?" on page 48 for more on eruptive emotions.)

2. HEAL: Identify dysfunctional patterns that were created from your Core Wounds and replace them with healthy patterns.

3. ATTRACT: Learn the skills on how to attract aligned experiences and opportunities into your life (such as your dream relationship, inner peace, your desired personal style, stronger communication, happiness).

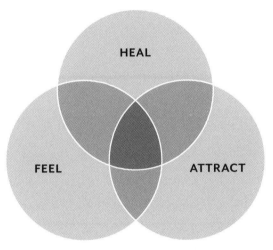

Now, I primarily use my Feel, Heal, Attract System™ with a reported 97 percent success in my program that helps women attract healthy relationships using inner-child healing.

However, it's also worked remarkably for other clients looking to heal from anxiety, depression, and other symptoms that result from childhood wounds. If you replace the romantic element with anything else you want to create your life (whether it's inner peace, healing, or confidence), it still works.

You'll notice that the heart of each pillar is similar to the 3 Stages of Recovery, in that it focuses on getting safe inside the body first. This is important! Healing without a steady, solid foundation can backfire. As we dive into each pillar in the following chapters, please do not skip ahead as each is meant to build on the previous ones.

Repeatedly over time, this same system has helped hundreds of my listeners go through the same stages of healing, no matter what goal they are working toward! Each pillar is absolutely crucial for any woman to thrive after a difficult childhood and to blossom into the best version of themselves.

So bestie, let's dive in and get you healed!

CHAPTER 7

PHASE 1: FEEL

"The emotion that can break your heart is sometimes the very one that heals it..."
—Nicholas Sparks, *At First Sight*

"YOU DON'T FUCKING LOVE ME."

The words almost screamed themselves as they escaped my lips.

I swiped the coffee cup off the table as my partner stood there, stunned speechless.

Big yikes. I already knew this was gonna be bad.

All he did was tell me that he was going to be away on a family trip for a few days. And yet, I reacted like a seven-year-old girl who was being abandoned all over again.

After the dust settled, I returned to being me again, remembering that he did indeed love me. But the damage was done. The insults had been hurled. Trust was breached.

This wasn't the first time that my own uncontrollable emotions had completely taken over and sabotaged a budding relationship. And until I found a way to deal with them better, no guy was going to survive trying to date me.

Basically what I'm trying to say is, I know the pain of feeling betrayed by your own emotions. And after many years, I've figured out the solution for both myself and my clients.

I call these tricky feelings "eruptive emotions." They are specific family groups of emotions that you have difficulty regulating or processing, which leads to feeling controlled by the emotions. This boils down to two things:

1. Hyperarousal: Intense, explosive, and reactive expression of certain emotions, feeling "out of control," sometimes described as being toddler-like. (Example: Suddenly throwing a tantrum due to anger.)

2. Hypoarousal: Repression or avoidance of certain emotions, numbing, "stuffing down." (Example: Judging your anger as "bad" and avoiding feeling it, or pretending it doesn't exist.)

Once you understand this concept, your life completely changes. You will be able to have control over something that once controlled you. And that is sweet, sweet magic!

WHY YOU'RE MORE REACTIVE THAN OTHER PEOPLE

"Parents' failures to empathize with their children, and the responses of their children to these failures, are at the root of almost all psychopathology."
—Heinz Kohut

You'd think that knowing how to deal with your feelings should be as instinctive as knowing how to breathe, right? Wrong!

Did you know that emotional regulation isn't something that kids naturally know how to do? Unlike things like breathing and sweating, humans actually need to be taught how to understand and deal with emotions from other people.

Just like learning to read and write, learning how to manage our emotions in a healthy way is something that needs to be demonstrated and role-modeled to us at an early age.

But the problem is actually deeply generational. After all, how are parents supposed to properly raise their children if *they themselves* were not taught these things?

You might have grown up watching your caregivers repress their feelings, cry hysterically, project their anger onto you, and throw tantrums like toddlers. It's just a sad situation overall, where emotionally stunted adults are raising emotionally stunted kids. Now it makes sense that your entire extended family seems really dysfunctional and immature. You were just copy-and-pasting each other's behavior. But it's never too late to end the cycle! Perhaps you were meant to be the one to put an end to it, once and for all.

SIGNS THAT YOUR CAREGIVERS WERE EMOTIONALLY IMMATURE (CHECKLIST)

○ Created a stressful home environment with unpredictable or volatile emotions
○ Were either very controlling or not caring at all
○ Showed very "hot and cold" behavior toward you
○ Got upset or passive-aggressive with you, but did not clearly communicate what the issue is
○ Avoided conflict by ignoring important issues (i.e., swept issues under the rug)

- ○ Never talked about emotions deeper than surface level
- ○ Had explosive tantrums that seemed toddler-like
- ○ Their mood instantly shifted from happy to cold to angry
- ○ Dismissed your emotions as wrong or unimportant
- ○ Overreacted to small things
- ○ The whole family rushed to soothe or appease the parent when they were upset
- ○ Took your emotions personally (e.g., Said things like, "Your anger is hurting my feelings.)
- ○ Felt triggered by your display of emotions (e.g., Told you to "Stop crying.")
- ○ You felt that you had to walk on eggshells to avoid upsetting them
- ○ You felt like you were the adult, and your parent was the child

---

This list can sometimes be shocking for people to read. Remember how we talked about your unmet needs within the four Core Wounds? Well, turns out our caregivers also have their own Core Wounds too.

This list can help validate that what you experienced growing up was real, and it actually had an impact on you. However, you may also have an uncomfortable realization that you also behave similarly to your parents. This is to be expected. None of us are immune from learning from our role models. However, you're the one reading this book and making a change toward healing and you should be so proud of this. That's something that your lineage probably didn't do.

ROLE REVERSAL

My client Anna had a very intertwined relationship with their mother. Anytime their mother was upset, Anna was at their beck and call. Anna would be the emotional punching bag and receive blame for everything that went wrong in their mother's life. They would pay for all of their mother's bills, drive them to doctor's appointments, and obey every request until their mother felt better. If Anna denied any request, they would be criticized for being selfish. Anna played many roles: the chauffeur, the therapist, the bank, the support worker. It seemed the only role they never got to play was that of daughter.

Sometimes an emotionally immature parent ends up depending on their own child for emotional support. The child ends up playing the role of the parent: They become the comforter and the soother, feeling responsible for their caregiver's emotions. This is called **parentification**. Remember that this was never supposed to be your job! You were the one who should have been protected, cared for, and soothed.

RETURNING TO THE BODY

Do you know why you have a body? It's not just a dumb meatbag for eating, sleeping, and repeating the cycle. The body has an intelligence of its own. It has built-in instincts and mysteries from millions of years of evolution. Your body is the vehicle that allows your consciousness to roam around the Earth to the best of its ability! Your body is truly remarkable machine that we can learn to love and take care of, with as much enthusiasm as some would have tending to vehicles like cars and bikes.

The next time you see a kid on the street, notice the absolute joy and freedom of how they express themselves with their bodies! Kids spin around, wave their limbs wildly, and dance spontaneously!

PRETEND TO BE A NEW SOUL

See what comes up for you when you pretend to be a new soul born into your body. What if you could capture the feeling of having a body for the first time? Pretend that having a body is a brand-new experience by following this step-by-step process:

1. Wiggle your fingers and toes.

2. Imagine your soul is "wearing" your hands like gloves, and feel the weight of your own body.

3. Breathe on your palms and notice the warmth you feel.

4. Stretch your arms safely (as much as you're able to), and feel how good it is to extend your body.

5. Place your hands on your head and notice the texture of your hair.

6. Take three deep breaths and notice how the air coming in is cool while the air going out is warm.

7. Stare at the rising and falling of your own chest and stomach as you breathe.

8. Jump onto a soft couch and notice your butt sinking into the cushion.

9. Wobble the loose part of your calves from side to side!

10. Tap your heels together playfully.

11. Shake your hips from side to side!

12. Finally, dance or move your body around, allowing it to do whatever it feels inspired to do!

How does your experience change after reconnecting with yourself and being aware of your physical body? What does your body want to do? I am a fan of spontaneous, ecstatic dance on a regular basis!

If you listen to your body, what wisdom can you learn from it?

_____

_____

_____

_____

_____

_____

_____

_____

_____

_____

_____

_____

_____

_____

_____

_____

WHAT ARE YOUR ERUPTIVE EMOTIONS?

It seems like we are constantly at war with our own emotions, feeling fearful or resistant toward something that is an important part of us. But what if emotions aren't as random and scary as they seem to be inside our heads? What if you only fear them because you haven't learned how to understand them? I help my students categorize their eruptive emotions into five specific family groups: mad, sad, glad, scared, and hurt. Seeing them clearly on paper, suddenly these students realize that feelings are *not* random and chaotic, but they actually have a way to make sense of how they feel!

The emotions in this chart are organized in ascending order of intensity. For example, grumpy feels a lot less intense than disgusted. Similarly, embarrassed isn't quite as heavy as ashamed. And fuzzy, glad feelings range from a subtle comfort all the way to ecstasy! Emotions are rich, beautiful, and deeply ingrained in the human experience.

Go through each column of emotions and give each word a score that corresponds with how comfortable you feel with that feeling **(1 = Avoid it, 2 = Uncomfortable, 3 = Accepting)**. The columns with your LOWEST average scores are your eruptive emotions that you can focus on getting in touch with the most.

MAD	#	SAD	#	GLAD	#
Mildly Irked		Disillusioned		Comfortable	
Irritated		Pessimistic		Relaxed	
Impatient		Disappointed		Calm	
Annoyed		Regretful		Trusting	
Frustrated		Sad		Content	
Grumpy		Tearful		Happy	
Spiteful		Shut down		Confident	
Disgusted		Paralyzed		Thankful	
Defensive		**Mournful**		**Joyful**	
Offended		**Depressed**		**Elated**	
Angry		**Grief**		**Excited**	
Rage		**Despair/Hopeless**		**Ecstatic**	

SCARED	#	HURT	#
Skeptical		Uncomfortable	
Cautious		Self-conscious	
Nervous		Isolated/lonely	
Mildly anxious		Vulnerable	
Confused		Embarrassed	
Worried		Victimized	
Preoccupied		Jealous	
Stressed		Betrayed	
Afraid		**Abandoned**	
Extremely anxious		**Inferior**	
Terrified		**Guilty**	
Petrified		**Pathetic**	
		Ashamed	

THE JEKYLL AND HYDE
BOSS-BABE WHO LIVED

One of my clients who took part in my Situationship to Soulmate program was an entrepreneur (let's call them "S"). S made an extraordinary discovery by doing the above exercise. They realized that *sad* was their comfort zone. They had grown up around a weepy mother and defaulted to crying whenever they were upset. However, it was *mad* that S truly struggled with. They grew up fearing raising their voice or being angry to avoid further upsetting their depressed mother. Without even realizing it, they developed a belief that "good girls don't get angry." Now, as an adult, all of their romantic relationships imploded. They tried to please men by being a "good girl," and eventually experienced spontaneous bursts of uncontrollable rage from all the bottled emotions rising up. It would shock them more than anyone else around them! Why, it was like they were Jekyll and Hyde!

Instead of randomly doing meditations and vaguely reminding them to "feel their feelings," I helped them only focus on the mad emotions that were causing them the most grief. Using the tools in the program, they were able to build a relationship with a really sweet guy without worrying about their emotions blowing up.

THE BUSY-BEE NURSE
WHO NEVER SMILED

Another client of mine, "T," was actually very comfortable with being sad, mad, and hurt! They were a busy-bee nurse whose schedule looked like a bad game of Tetris. Turns out it was glad feelings that made them deeply uncomfortable. They had lost their sister in a tragic accident at a young age and proceeded to spend their life denying themselves of pleasure. If they were too happy, it made them feel guilty for the happiness their sister never got to experience. If they were too relaxed, it reminded them of the calm before the storm right before that terrible car accident occurred. They were afraid of happiness. And so, they remained busy and overbooked, and felt it was easier to remain miserable instead.

T learned that despite what happened to their sister, they were allowed to bathe in the light again. They realized that their sister would have wanted them to keep living their life, and that their love was eternal. T made a new commitment to carry on the legacy of their sister's smile through their own story.

ANGER AS A "MASKING" EMOTION

Sometimes emotions actually cover deeper hidden emotions, and anger is usually one of those culprits. Yes, anger is absolutely valid as its own emotion. However, you might also find that some people find it easier to get angry when deep down, they're actually hurt.

In some families and cultures, displaying anger is more socially acceptable than the more vulnerable feelings associated with "weakness," such as sadness. In very old-school masculine culture, for example, men are ridiculed for crying. This can also apply to women. Do you remember hearing the phrase "big girls don't cry"? The whole thing is so messed up and untrue. I truly hope that this is something that we unlearn as a society.

JOURNAL PROMPTS

MAD

1. What's your earliest memory of feeling mad?

Example: The memory I have of feeling angry is of the first time my mother denied saying mean things to me. I was overcome with rage, and I remember "seeing red."

2. How did your family members deal with feeling mad? What did you learn from this? Who are you most similar to?

Example: I see my similarities with father. My father would drink after work hours, and would rage at my mother and me. It was scarier when I was young, and as I got older I would yell back at him. I think I learned to believe that anger was a negative emotion that I didn't want to associate with.

3. Was there a pattern with mad emotions in your family?

Example: Everything appeared to be calm in the family until my father became drunk. It turned into a cycle of him getting angry, my mother pleading with him and crying, and then a period where it got swept under the rug.

4. Do you fear this emotion?

Example: Yes, I'm afraid that feeling angry will lead me to hurting people.

5. How did you deal with mad feelings as a child?

Example: As a child, I bottled it up and drew angry drawings.

6. How do you deal with your mad feelings now?

Example: I find that I still bottle up my mad feelings as an adult. It never works, as eventually I explode.

7. What beliefs do you carry about this emotion (consciously or unconsciously)?

Example: I think I associate the emotion of anger with my alcoholic father, and I think I'm becoming him when I feel anger. However, now I understand that anger is a natural human emotion. Just because my father expressed it in a very unhealthy way doesn't mean that I need to do the same.

SAD

1. What's your earliest memory of feeling sad?

Example: After grandmother passed away.

2. How did your family members deal with feeling sad? What did you learn from this? Who are you most similar to?

Example: My mother was frequently sad and sulking, and I see myself in them. I learned that as a woman, sad should be my default state.

3. Was there a pattern with sad emotions in your family?

Example: Whenever my father would have a depression episode, he would expect me to take care of him, and that made me feel guilty.

_____

_____

_____

_____

4. Do you fear this emotion?

Example: I'm afraid of burdening people with sadness the way my father used it against me.

_____

_____

_____

_____

5. How did you deal with sad feelings as a child?

Example: I would cry in private and try to keep it to myself.

_____

_____

_____

_____

6. How do you deal with your sad feelings now?

Example: I still struggle to cry, or automatically repress sad feelings.

_____

_____

_____

_____

7. What beliefs do you carry about this emotion (consciously or unconsciously)?

Example: Because it makes me uncomfortable, I think I believe that sadness makes me weak because of how my father dealt with it.

GLAD

1. What's your earliest memory of feeling glad?

Example: I remember feeling so excited and happy during my first birthday party, when I felt really special.

---

2. How did your family members deal with feeling glad? What did you learn from this? Who are you most similar to?

Example: I'm pretty similar to my grandmother, who naturally likes to giggle at silly things. They made me feel safe.

---

3. Was there a pattern with glad emotions in your family?

Example: Because things were always up and down in the house, joy and laughter always felt like the calm before the storm. It never lasted long.

4. Do you fear this emotion?

Example: In some ways, yes. I'm afraid to let myself fully feel happiness and joy, because I'm afraid of feeling crushed if it goes away. I find myself holding back about 50 percent of the time.

5. How did you deal with glad feelings as a child?

Example: As a child, joyful feelings were a relief for me and I actively sought them out.

6. How do you deal with your glad feelings now?

Example: I do find myself holding back now, as if to prevent getting used to happiness. The only time I can freely experience joy is when I'm with a loved one.

7. What beliefs do you carry about this emotion (consciously or unconsciously)?

Example: I have a belief that letting myself feel too happy will set me up for disappointment. However, that's not what I really want. I would like to live a full life with no regrets.

SCARED

1. What's your earliest memory of feeling scared?

Example: I got separated from my parents in a mall during a busy holiday weekend, and I felt terrified and paralyzed. I couldn't even move. When security eventually reunited us, my mom yelled at me in public instead of consoling me. It was an awful feeling.

2. How did your family members deal with feeling scared? What did you learn from this? Who are you most similar to?

Example: In our family, sometimes people would react with anger when they were actually afraid. They did not do well with vulnerable feelings, and I feel I am similar to all of these people. I learned that it's not okay to admit that you feel scared, or that I need to always try to be strong.

3. Was there a pattern with scared emotions in your family?

Example: My family had lots of hidden anxiety and jittery vibes, with nobody ever acknowledging or expressing their fears in a healthy way.

_____

_____

_____

_____

_____

4. Do you fear this emotion?

Example: I'm becoming better at accepting anxiety and fear.

_____

_____

_____

_____

_____

5. How did you deal with scared feelings as a child?

Example: As a child, I felt shamed and rejected for these feelings, and I would cry.

_____

_____

_____

_____

_____

6. How do you deal with your scared feelings now?

Example: I notice that I sometimes react similarly to how my parents did.

_____

_____

_____

_____

_____

7. What beliefs do you carry about this emotion (consciously or unconsciously)?

Example: I think I have a deeper belief that being anxious or scared is not something I'm allowed to display to other people. I have an instinct to push it away, when really I should try to feel the emotion.

HURT

1. What's your earliest memory of feeling hurt?

Example: My earliest memory of hurt was telling my older brother that I was being bullied at school, and him laughing in my face about it. It then also made me feel ashamed of admitting it, and I felt like I somehow deserved it.

2. How did your family members deal with feeling hurt? What did you learn from this? Who are you most similar to?

Example: Both of my parents never discussed or showed that they were hurt, and I see myself in both of them. They would give each other the silent treatment and sweep issues under the rug, only for them to fester and breed resentment. What I learned was that you're not allowed to tell people that you're hurt, that it's something to keep hidden.

3. Was there a pattern with hurt emotions in your family?

Example: My mother would always get offended and hurt about something small, which would lead to my father becoming sad and trying to please them. I can see myself enacting this pattern from both sides.

4. Do you fear this emotion?

Example: Because my mother always needed to be the victim, I was never allowed to feel more hurt than them. I don't fear the emotion, but I repress it.

5. How did you deal with hurt feelings as a child?

Example: As a child, I tried to minimize the hurt to avoid offending my mother.

6. How do you deal with your hurt feelings now?

Example: I find that I downplay my own feelings or try to convince myself that they're not worth causing a fuss over. This leads to me feeling resentful when my needs aren't met.

7. What beliefs do you carry about this emotion (consciously or unconsciously)?

Example: I think I have unconscious beliefs that my hurts aren't as bad or as serious as other people's, or that I don't deserve to express them.

_____

_____

_____

_____

_____

YOU MUST *FEEL IT* TO *HEAL IT*

Ugh, the tears.

My legs trembled, my whole torso shook violently as tears poured like waterfalls down my cheeks as I sat on my therapist's leather couch. That was the first time I allowed somebody to see the real me as I poured my heart out about the love I didn't feel as a little girl.

And as I bared my soul, my therapist's kind words reached into the youngest part of me, showing me that it was okay to break down. That it was okay to feel. That these emotions would not kill me or last forever, no matter how big they felt.

What I learned later in life is that emotions aren't something to be scared of. This is a humbling wisdom that I will continue coming back to, probably for the rest of my life!

As it turns out, the way to stabilize your eruptive emotions is to learn how to *feel* and regulate your emotions properly. Imagine being in harmony and feeling in control of your emotions. Many of my students have achieved this, and it's possible for you too! But first we need to understand the purpose of our emotions.

EMOTIONS ARE OUR GREATEST TEACHERS

Emotions are *signals*, sort of like those of a GPS. Emotions show us what we like, what we don't like, and what parts of us still need healing. They are the gateway to our authentic selves and souls. Emotions give our lives meaning. Every joyful song in existence, every moving piece of art etched into stone, was birthed from the deepest of human emotions.

Emotions cannot be controlled or deleted. They can only be felt, processed, and fully released through the body.

The body never forgets. Any emotions you push away or resist will inevitably resurface as an explosion, or manifest as health concerns.

As the saying goes, "What you resist, persists."

HOW TO *ACTUALLY* FEEL YOUR FEELINGS

Everyone and their neighbor talks about "sitting with feelings," but most people aren't doing it properly. Let's take a look at this:

THINGS THAT ARE NOT FEELING YOUR FEELINGS:

- Doing yoga
- Noticing your emotions during a meditation
- Rage-venting to someone
- Emotionally eating with ice cream

What is happening here? While all of these activities can help us *identify* and *talk about* the emotions, they are not focused on truly feeling and surrendering to those feelings. The majority of people with inner-child wounds still operate emotionally like a toddler who never grew up.

In order to truly feel your feelings, you must let go of resistance, repression, and judgment. You must experience the emotion genuinely and let it run its course, naturally exiting your body. You cannot secretly wish for the feeling to go away faster or try to control it. There cannot be any ulterior motive other than giving the emotion permission to do what it needs.

In fact, over many years, I've learned that my clients are *thinking* about sitting with their feelings, not actually *feeling* them! They do this because it creates the illusion that they're doing something about it, when really it's more comfortable just to stay in the thinking mind instead of getting into the body. As I mentioned earlier, your body is your vehicle and your home. It's time to reclaim your home!

WHAT REALLY HAPPENS WHEN YOU PUSH DOWN YOUR EMOTIONS

A lot of us grow up with this false belief that being strong and ignoring your feelings will make them go away. Right? Dead wrong.

I'm going to use a gross analogy to really bring the point home. Pushing down your emotions is like holding in your farts. It may relieve you of the temporary discomfort of being a Smelly Nelly. But where is that trapped gas actually going? It's not disappearing into thin air. In fact, the pressure simply retains and builds gas within your digestive system, which can lead to pain, bloating, and heartburn.

When you hold in your feelings, you are also sacrificing temporary discomfort for long-term damage to your emotional and physical health. And that's because it takes considerable energy and resources for your body to continuously repress emotions that are trying to bubble up to the surface. Have you ever tried not to laugh when you were thinking about something funny, to the point that you couldn't even focus on what was being said in the conversation? That's what you're putting your body through every day as it eats up your energy trying to bury feelings. Then you go home and wonder why you feel so much more exhausted than everybody else.

WHAT YOU RESIST, PERSISTS

Resistance can double or even triple the intensity of the emotion you're feeling! Let's say your anxiety level is at a 4/10 in terms of intensity. Meaning, if you let yourself feel it right now, it would only feel like a 4.

"I'm anxious."

But, then, let's say you judge the emotion. You think, "I *hate* feeling anxious." The resistance behind thinking that thought adds a secondary layer of anger.

Now, the intensity level rises to a 6/10.

"I <u>hate</u> feeling anxious."

Finally, let's say you then try to push away the feelings of anxiety-mixed-with-anger and begin fighting with your own mind. You think, "Fine, I'll try to feel this stupid feeling so that hopefully it goes away and never comes back."

"Fine, I'll try to feel this stupid feeling so it goes away and never comes back!!!"

Suddenly, you're at an 8/10 intensity. It's nearly double what you started with, simply because you've stacked layers of this resistance. All of the stacking makes it feel a lot heavier on you, doesn't it?

As you continue improving your emotional skills, it's best to nip things in the budding stage before they build up and fester over time. This is something that takes trial-and-error practice over time, so don't sweat it if you can't do it at first!

JOURNAL PROMPTS

1. What am I unwilling to *feel* right now?

_____

_____

_____

_____

2. What have I been taught about staying strong as a woman? Why might these beliefs be true or untrue?

_____

_____

_____

_____

3. What have I learned about my feelings not being important or worthy of being witnessed and expressed? Why isn't this true?

_____

_____

_____

_____

4. When I was growing up, did my family members hold in their feelings?

_____

_____

_____

_____

DON'T WORRY, THEY DON'T LAST FOREVER

Brain scientist Dr. Jill Bolte Taylor suggests in their book *A Stroke of Insight,* that it only takes 90 seconds to identify and dissipate an emotion, otherwise known as the "90-second rule." But, really, when's the last time one of your intense feelings *only* lasted a minute and half, even with your conscious effort to shift it? In my experience, people who struggle with eruptive emotions don't have enough experience properly regulating their emotions and aren't able to benefit from the 90-second rule right away (Bolte, 2008).

What I've found for clients I've worked with, is that the peak intensity of emotions can last 90 *minutes* rather than seconds at first! However, with practice comes improvement. If you allow intense emotions to be *fully* felt, they often will naturally begin to decline after around the 90-minute mark. Eventually, the peak intensity will become shorter.

This is the best news ever. Why? Because it means that no matter how deep, spiraling, or painful an emotion is, the peak of that intensity will never last forever. Sometimes people are afraid that allowing themselves to feel bad means they'll be trapped in it forever. Ironically, this might only happen if you're resisting the emotion.

Trust that your body has a natural intelligence that can regulate itself, but only if you allow it to do its job. Sweating ends when the body cools down. Hunger is curbed when the stomach receives food. The body is exhausted of serotonin and hormones after an emotion runs its full course.

LIFESPAN OF INTENSE EMOTIONS

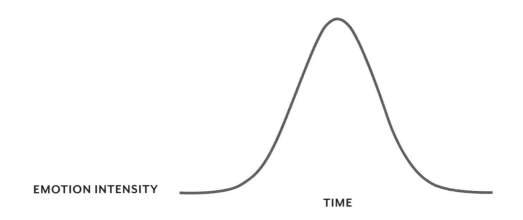

EMOTION INTENSITY

TIME

THE EMOTIONAL BACKLOG

If you have years of repressed emotions that are bursting at the seams, it may take longer than 90 minutes for them to ease up at the beginning. It will also be difficult to intentionally feel happy and joy, because those feelings are being blocked off by this "backlog" of feelings that are begging to be expressed and released!

Think of "happy emotions" as gold that fills up a mine. There's nothing inherently stopping you from experiencing them. However, all of that unfelt and unresolved grief, anger, hurt, and sadness is plugging up the entrance. It takes time and patience to work through this.

However, with gentleness, you'll find that the next time you embrace that emotion, the peak will end in 50 minutes. And then 30 minutes. And then 7 minutes. Until you finally feel like you've got a grip on this!

They say that violence begets violence. In a similar fashion, fighting your emotions only creates more fighting. Surrendering to your emotions creates more surrender.

Which one do you want to choose?

THE SACRED RELEASE

I've had a lot of relationships and situationships that did not work out. In each case, the exact same thing would happen.

I'd buy an entire McCain Deep'n Delicious cake for myself (the chocolate kind, of course), and a bottle of red wine. I would proceed to drink my sorrows away while distracting myself with YouTube videos of meditations.

One night, a profound realization hit me during a drunken stupor, while Whitney's "I Have Nothing" played on repeat as I lay on the living room floor, a tenderness blooming inside me.

It clicked that by distracting myself with drinking, with cake, and with YouTube videos, I was precisely *not* feeling my feelings. I realized that even meditation was a distraction in these moments.

Because the purpose of my seeking alcohol, meditation, and music was motivated by making the bad feelings go away, I wasn't truly honoring them. Which means, I wasn't truly feeling them.

By trying to feel better quickly, I was actually telling my inner girl that her feelings were too inconvenient for me, that they didn't matter. That I couldn't handle them, and they were big and needed to be nipped and shrunk away. And that thread translated into something bigger and deeper: *That, somehow, I was too big and inconvenient and needed to be shrunk away.*

I suddenly felt so sad for Little Gloria and the way I'd treated her feelings.

And as Whitney kept belting her heart out in the background, I had an even more sacred experience. I realized that all the great artists in human history felt the exact same emotions that I did. Sorrow. Grief. Perseverance. That despite the pain of the emotions, there was also beauty in their existence. Feeling the emotions meant that I was human and that I was alive, feeling what my fellow souls have also felt.

So, I shut off the music. I closed the laptop, tucked away the bottle. And for two hours, I sat fully present with little me, *feeling without any resistance,* cradling myself and crying into my own arms until there were no more tears left.

I woke up the next morning like a brand-new woman. Something ancient had finally been lifted from my body. I named this practice of feeling your feelings the "Sacred Release," because that's what it really felt like for me. It was sacred, spiritual, and freeing.

RULES FOR DOING A SACRED RELEASE (AKA, FEELING YOUR FEELINGS)

1. No matter how big your feelings are, they will not hurt or kill you.

2. Don't have an ulterior motive to get rid of your emotions or make them go by faster.

3. Set aside two hours in order get through the emotional peak, trusting that the emotion needs to fully run its course.

4. Plan to surround yourself with comforting items such as cozy pajamas, socks, and warm tea in order to create a safe place for feeling.

5. Allow yourself to fully *feel* the emotion inside your body, without resistance or trying to hold back.

6. Gentle is powerful. Don't be hard on yourself if you struggle at first. As with all things, it takes gentleness and practice.

CAN'T CRY? SOME CRYING TIPS

1. Start your Sacred Release session by playing sad or emotional music that can help activate your feelings. Once they're open, focus on the emotions themselves.

2. Watch a clip of a movie that's always made you cry in the past.

3. Make crying sounds or pretend to cry. Sometimes going through the motions of the behavior can help to activate real tears.

4. Draw a picture of your inner-child crying.

Now that we've narrowed down *which* emotions you are having trouble with, you can breathe a sigh of relief! Isn't it nice to have fewer and more specific things to work on?

JOURNAL REFLECTION

1. How were you treated as a child when you cried? How did that impact you?

2. What's your current relationship with crying? What would you like to change about it?

WHY GRATITUDE CAN FEEL LIKE GASLIGHTING

While the practice of gratitude can be a wonderful tool in cultivating happiness, there's a reason it can backfire at the start of your journey.

Many of us have had our emotions belittled and dismissed. We might remember the words that accompany a wagging finger: "Why can't you just be GRATEFUL for what you have?" instead of compassion and understanding for how we were actually feeling. Many of us grew up resenting that word "gratitude" because it was weaponized against us to make us feel guilty. Therefore, forcibly trying to be grateful is just another way of dismissing your valid feelings. Except now you are doing it to yourself!

If someone was rude to you, then it makes perfect sense to feel upset rather than grateful. If your pet passed away, then of course you'd feel grief instead of gratitude. How you feel is how you feel. There is no such thing as a good or bad feeling, as they are all valid. So why should we force ourselves to feel grateful when we really don't feel that way? Why should we downplay or censor our truth, just to make another person comfortable? Some people would rather flip the blame on you, cover their ears, because it threatens their belief that they're such a great person instead of acknowledging that maybe they did something wrong. That is not the vibe of gratitude.

In fact, you'll find that *true* gratitude is not a feeling that needs to be forced. When you are taking care of your inner-child and respecting your own emotions, gratitude will naturally bubble up when it's genuine. So, stop chasing emotions and focus on accepting the emotions that are already present. We need to work through dirt before reaching gold.

IT'S IMPOSSIBLE TO THINK WHEN YOU'RE TRIGGERED

"I had a fight with my fiancée again, and I just totally froze up. I WANTED to use my communication skills. I WANTED to open my mouth and move my arms, but I couldn't. I feel so frustrated and helpless at my own body. How can I react better when I'm triggered?"

This paraphrases a very common question I get at least once a year when I'm working with my clients. My response?

You can't! Because when emotions trigger us into a survival response, it's virtually *impossible to learn anything new OR think rationally.*

It's involuntary. The front part of your brain that does all the thinking goes offline. Your body believes it's in danger and does everything it thinks is necessary to protect you.

Many women I've worked with spent years hating their bodies for reacting, when all this time their bodies had been their saving grace.

So take a deep breath, bestie. Let that reach the corners of your body. Don't blame yourself for something outside of your control.

Your body and brain love you *so* much, that they're pulling out all stops for you. In these moments, all we can do is remain gentle with our inner girls and regulate ourselves.

This idea of how our nervous systems are involved with feelings of safety are described in polyvagal theory, which was popularized by psychologist Dr. Stephen Porges. Below is a diagram inspired by the ideas behind polyvagal theory, which can help you understand why your body responds in certain ways depending on how you feel (Porges, 2022).

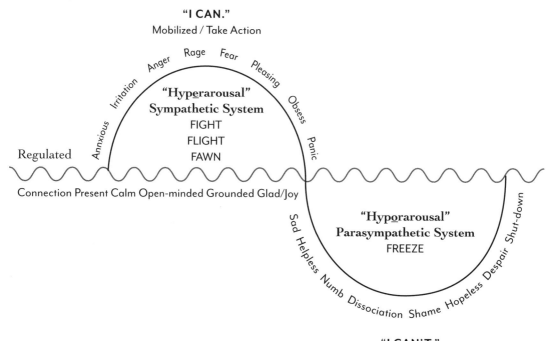

"I CAN."
Mobilized / Take Action

Anger Rage Fear
Irritation Pleasing
Anxious Obsess
"Hyperarousal"
Sympathetic System
FIGHT
FLIGHT
Panic
FAWN

Regulated

Connection Present Calm Open-minded Grounded Glad/Joy

Sad Helpless Numb Dissociation Shame Hopeless Despair Shut-down

"Hypoarousal"
Parasympathetic System
FREEZE

"I CAN'T."
Immobilized /
Emergency Deactivation

WHAT TO DO INSTEAD WHEN YOU FEEL TRIGGERED

Now that you understand that you literally can't immediately respond clearly when triggered, the solution is to provide your inner-child a safe place until the storm passes. The quicker you allow for the process, the faster you'll return to a regulated baseline.

If you observe the diagram above, you'll be able to determine when you are feeling hyperarousal versus hypoarousal.

Hyperarousal is characterized by intensity, big feelings, obsession, and panic. Hypoarousal, on the other end, feels numb, disconnected, hopeless, and shut down.

WHAT TO DO IF YOU'RE HYPERAROUSED

An activated sympathetic nervous system makes you feel like you're in crisis.

It makes you feel anxious. It makes you feel urgent and intense. It can sometimes make you feel like your body moves on its own. It can feel like your words rapidly speak themselves, before your mind even has a chance to think.

You may experience the urge to fight and defend yourself. You may feel the urge to escape and run away. Or, you may feel an extreme impulse to obsess, beg, plead, or appease the other person. All of these feelings are normal for a bodily system that was designed to protect you at all costs.

The first step is to not judge yourself for feeling this way, and identify how you are feeling on the diagram above (for example, *I am feeling obsessive about this event and seem to be in hyperarousal*).

The second step is to expend all of this adrenaline through a healthy outlet. All of that heightened energy needs to be moved and released through your body! Some great ways to do this include going for a run, dancing, yoga, safely punching a pillow, screaming, and stretching your body.

Some people are afraid of expressing the fight response, because they are afraid of becoming violent like their abusers. I want to reassure you that this is not going to happen! The fight response is a mechanism that evolved as a way for our ancestors to defend themselves in the past. It's a part of who you are. There is a huge difference between honoring one's natural protective instincts in a healthy way versus intentionally directing pain at innocent victims.

WHAT TO DO IF YOU'RE HYPOAROUSED

Activation of the parasympathetic nervous system, on the other hand, feels like a shutdown.

It feels numb. It feels slow, hazy, frozen, helpless. At its worst, it can feel like complete despair. It can feel like a fog has taken over and your mind is unable to see the good in anything. You may feel the urge to disconnect from people around you.

It can also feel psychedelic or spiritual, with a strange sensation that you are not inside your body. This type of dissociation can happen when your body doesn't feel safe to live inside.

As with hyperarousal, shutting down is another way that your body has evolved to try to protect you from harm. For example, rabbits exhibit a freeze response by pretending to be dead in order to increase their chances of survival from a predator. Although humans no longer need defending from wildlife threats, we actually use this type of protection in modern-day situations.

Again, please do not blame yourself for feeling this way. It's an involuntary response.

When your body goes into deactivation, it won't help to run around as if you were in hyperarousal. Instead, do the opposite!

Try small, soft movements to gently invite your inner-child to become present inside your body again. Some ideas to include all five senses include taking a warm bath, giving yourself a hand massage using scented lotions, drinking warm tea or soup, curling up in a cozy blanket, listening to calming music or nature sounds, or watching videos of relaxing landscapes.

TRIGGER CHEAT SHEET

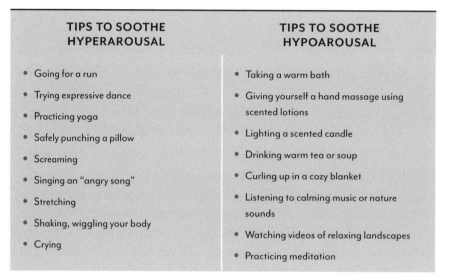

TIPS TO SOOTHE HYPERAROUSAL	TIPS TO SOOTHE HYPOAROUSAL
• Going for a run	• Taking a warm bath
• Trying expressive dance	• Giving yourself a hand massage using scented lotions
• Practicing yoga	• Lighting a scented candle
• Safely punching a pillow	• Drinking warm tea or soup
• Screaming	• Curling up in a cozy blanket
• Singing an "angry song"	• Listening to calming music or nature sounds
• Stretching	• Watching videos of relaxing landscapes
• Shaking, wiggling your body	• Practicing meditation
• Crying	

JOURNAL REFLECTION

1. How does your body react when you feel triggered or overwhelmed? Try to describe the sensations in detail.

_____

_____

_____

2. Do you tend to go into hyperarousal or hypoarousal? What's your earliest memory of reacting this way?

_____

_____

3. In what situations do you go into hyperarousal? In what situations do you go into hypoarousal?

_____

_____

_____

4. Using the tips above, what are some ways you can implement these suggestions to soothe your hyperarousal or hypoarousal?

_____

_____

_____

TIPS FOR DEALING WITH NUMBNESS

Try this technique if your body continues to feel numb. Look at your own hand and say out loud to yourself, "It is safe to feel my pinky." With that intention, allow yourself to feel the sensation of moving your pinky. Then move onto the next finger, and the next. Then, feel your entire hand, and then your entire arm. Continue working your way up until you allow yourself to sit in your entire body.

GIRL, LET IT ALL OUT

I worked with a sweet woman named Cora who worked with kids in the health-care industry. They would happily chortle and gab about all the other people in their life. But every time I asked their opinion on something, they would clam up like a shell. This pattern made our interactions very limited, but Cora was determined to get to the bottom of what was preventing them from opening up.

After some digging, we discovered that Cora was never asked their opinion when they were growing up. Their father was the stereotypical stronghold of the family who made all of the decisions. And by decisions, I meant _all_ of the decisions, including what Cora was to wear to school, what extracurricular activities he deemed appropriate, and even what friends he found acceptable. Though it was never vocally expressed, Cora was discouraged from disagreeing or even showing disappointment about these choices. They never had a voice! This was a huge light bulb moment for Cora as they realized that they actually had many emotions about things! Slowly, over time, Cora was able to give themselves permission to speak up at work and in her relationships.

HOW YOU REALLY FEEL

Now, it's your turn! Answer these questions honestly.

How You Feel about Yourself:

How do you feel about yourself as a person?

What's your favorite thing about yourself?

How do you feel about expressing your emotions and opinions?

What is your favorite physical feature?

How do you honestly feel when you're engaging in your hobbies?

How do you honestly feel about your sexuality?

How do you honestly feel about "failure"?

How do you honestly feel about "success"?

What makes you feel happy?

What makes you feel sad?

What makes you feel stressed?

What makes you feel scared?

What makes you feel angry?

What makes you feel hurt?

How You Feel about Others:

How do you feel about your family of origin?

How do you feel when you are with your friends?

How do you feel when you are at work or around coworkers?

How do you feel about your neighbors?

How do you feel in high-energy, crowded places?

How do you feel in low-energy, quieter places?

How do you feel when people compliment you?

How do you feel when others are very loud and chatty?

How do you feel when others are quiet and soft-spoken?

How do you feel about men?

How do you feel about women?

How do you feel about sex and intimacy?

How do you feel about love?

How You Feel about the World:

How do you feel about living in your current neighborhood?

How do you feel about living in your city?

How do you feel about the current politics/government?

How do you feel about money?

What kind of environment makes you feel the safest?

How do you feel about the universe/your spiritual beliefs?

JOURNAL PROMPTS

1. Were you surprised by any of your honest answers? Why or why not?

2. What has been holding you back from expressing your truth?

CHAPTER 8

PHASE 2: HEAL

"Children don't get traumatized because they are hurt.
They get traumatized because they're alone with the hurt."
—Dr. Gabor Maté

You've made it this far, love!

At this point in your journey, you've had some a-ha moments when discovering which Core Wounds you carried from childhood. You've also started rebuilding your relationship with your emotions and taken back your power. These emotional-regulation skills are going to come in handy in this chapter as we explore the hard stuff.

Phase 2 isn't easy. In fact, it will probably consist of some of the hardest work you've ever done. Nobody said that facing your past and healing it was going to be a walk in the park. But compared to the suffering you're currently going through, isn't it worth it?

The temporary pain of healing is still easier than living the rest of your life exactly how it's currently going. In my experience, living your life in denial is hard. Having no boundaries and experiencing breakdowns every week is hard. Being stuck in toxic relationships for years and feeling depleted and rejected… is hard. Your life is already hard. So, are you open to experiencing a temporary period of increased challenges if it means you can live the rest of your life in ease?

On the other side of healing is this: Peaceful relationships. Fulfillment and freedom. Unapologetic confidence. Joy and happiness. Now *that* is the kind of easy I can get used to!

The healing phase is something that takes much longer than a weekend, especially when you don't have accountability to see things through. That's why I run group-based programs so that I can hold your hand and help you cross the finish line. Even my programs run between months to a year! This is because I know that it takes a while to fully integrate these teachings and embody a new way of existing. Also, new problems are sometimes created after doing the healing process. For example, after healing, it's normal for clients to suddenly begin attracting many potential partners and opportunities and want help adjusting to this new normal of abundance.

Trust that you already have the ability to do challenging things! You've already made it through so many difficult things before. You are deeply capable and powerful. With self-compassion and patience, you will absolutely find your way through.

THE CHOICE PENDULUM

As you go through these re-parenting chapters, you'll realize that healing sometimes feels contradictory.

"Am I supposed to take a break when it feels hard, or am I just avoiding the work?'"

"Are my boundaries reasonable, or am I just putting up a wall?"

"Is it self-care to take a nap when I'd feel more relieved just doing the dishes now?"

What I've come to accept is that nobody other than yourself can give you the right answer. It is only through trial and error that you will discover what is best for *you*.

For example, I often see articles encouraging women to dye their hair brilliant colors as a way to empower themselves. This is a great message! I'm very happy for these women who may have grown up conservatively and are finally doing what they want. Coach Ashton Williams, one of the support coaches who works with me inside my programs, is one of these women who sports an edgy bright red that looks fantastic on them! It was a huge breakthrough for them to change their look after being raised to look like a Barbie doll. But this would not be empowering for me. When I was a teenager facing my abandonment wounds, I used wild hair color as a way to put more eyes on me. Since I hated my real hair, it was coming from a place of self-loathing and not empowerment! In fact, it took me a long time to learn to love my natural jet-black locks and truly believe that I am enough just as myself. Although Coach Ashton and I took different journeys, we still arrived at the same place of self-love. So you see, the same action can be empowering for one woman and disempowering for another. You are the only one who can decide what's true for you!

To simplify this idea for you, I'm going to use the metaphor of a pendulum.

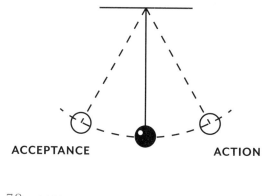

ACCEPTANCE   ACTION

You'll notice that one end of the pendulum says acceptance and the other side is labeled action. Life is a constant dance between making these two decisions.

Acceptance is when you realize it's time to soften, surrender, accept, or make peace with something. My hair color is an example of this, because this choice stemmed from an inner knowing that it was time to stop running away from myself and stop changing my hair!

Action is when you realize that you need to *do something* in order to be in alignment with your truth. Coach Ashton realized that they couldn't repress their desire for unicorn-colored hair in order to please their relatives, and their choice came from a place of inspiration. Picking up this book and doing these exercises is another example of taking action!

There's a lot of "gurus" out there who insist that there's only one right way to deal with life's problems. Don't listen to these people. In fact, run as fast as you can from anybody who is trying to tell you what to think instead of *how to think*.

Let's go through some common examples to help you discover your truth!

EXAMPLE: FEELING OVERWHELMED AT YOUR DIRTY DISH PILE

Option 1: Do you have a pattern of overworking yourself, perfectionism, or beating yourself up over a couple of messy dishes? If so, you may choose acceptance as a way to practice imperfection and give yourself a break.

Option 2: Do you have a pattern of not taking care of yourself or procrastinating on tasks until they become unmanageable? Are you actually overwhelmed due to lack of energy or do you want to avoid chores? If so, you might choose action as a way to practice self-care and start building better habits.

EXAMPLE: ENDING A RELATIONSHIP WITH AN ANNOYING FRIEND

Option 1: Do you have a pattern of cutting people off immediately or avoiding confrontation and difficult conversations? Do you have a habit of nitpicking at people's flaws as a defense mechanism? If so, you might consider acceptance and use this opportunity to talk to your friend about it first and practice accepting their personality.

Option 2: Do you have a pattern of putting up with other people's behavior and dismissing your own feelings? Has a friend repeatedly disrespected you despite your vocalization? If so, you might choose action and end the relationship as an opportunity to set boundaries and take care of yourself.

See how the solution depends on your unique history? Whereas one person should set a boundary, another person might need to have a chat instead.

PRACTICING YOUR CHOICE PENDULUM

Take time to brainstorm ideas on how you might deal with the following situations based on your own needs:

1. Your aunt is rambling on about politics at Thanksgiving.

Acceptance: _____

Action: _____

2. It's your third attempt to climb the wall at the rock climbing gym, and you feel extremely frustrated.

Acceptance: _____

Action: _____

3. Someone cut in front of you at the grocery store line.

Acceptance: _____

Action: _____

4. You're writing a poem and can't think of any ideas.

Acceptance: _____

Action: _____

5. Your in-laws are coming over in two hours, but the house is a mess.

Acceptance: _____

Action: _____

6. It's the second time your best friend canceled at the last minute.

Acceptance: _____

Action: _____

CHOICE CREATES CLARITY

My client Hailey was ruminating about a Friday night decision: "I feel sluggish and I'm not sure if I should go out with friends or stay in and watch a movie. I know that sometimes I instantly feel better when I'm actually out the door. What should I do?"

When the pendulum isn't a clear left or right, it will most certainly *become clear* after you make a choice. Any choice!

They chose to take action and went out to meet their friends. Upon arriving at the scene, it became instantly clear that they were not feeling the vibe of the café. So, they went home instead and watched reruns of *The Fresh Prince of Bel-Air*. On a different day, however, it's also possible that they could have loved the café and chosen to stay.

The point is that you're not going to suddenly become enlightened by sitting still and twiddling your thumbs. If you're waffling between two decisions, just close your eyes and pick one. Then, adjust your decision accordingly.

JOURNAL PROMPTS

Reflect on these questions when you are having a hard time making a decision. This exercise may require setting your journal aside, and returning later to reflect on a choice that has been made.

1. If you feel torn between two choices, which one can you just decide to go with?

2. What was the result of that choice? What does this information tell you about how you would like to deal with this situation in the future?

TRUTH DEFIES LOGIC!

Sometimes, your unique choice might go against what everyone else thinks. One of my private clients also hosts an incredible podcast that has been taking off recently. In fact, they were the first person in their family to take the path less traveled and transition from a comfortable job to starting a business. And boy, did they have opinions! They called their reckless. They called their decision irresponsible and illogical. They begged them to change their mind, and not once did they take the time to understand why this business was so important to them.

The truth is that when you start making choices for yourself, some people will never understand. We all grow up with a story of what milestones we're "supposed" to hit throughout life, and it can threaten people's beliefs to color outside of those lines. I experienced the same thing when I spent my savings account to do a month of solo travel and ayahuasca retreats in South America. I was told that I was making a huge mistake and wasting my money. During the trip, I burst into tears and started to wonder if those criticisms could be true. After all, I had just graduated from college and didn't have a job! During the trip, I fell into regret and started to believe that I should have listened to the doubters.

However, the perspective I gained from that trip shifted the direction of my entire life and eventually led to me starting my podcast and then writing this book. It took almost seven years to look back and realize that everything I have now was due to that decision I made to get on that plane. What people didn't know at the time is that my living situation back then was very toxic. Small, comfortable changes weren't enough to break me out of my shell. It was only through a dramatic change in environment that the life-changing idea was able to form in my head: "What if I learned more about my inner-child, and maybe even helped other people do the same?" Fast forward a few years later, I'm so glad I made that "stupid" decision, and I don't care that people disagreed. It was worth every penny, and I'm the only one laughing in the end!

JOURNAL PROMPTS

1. Have you ever made a decision that defied what others told you? What happened afterwards?

_____

_____

_____

_____

2. Is there a decision you need to make right now that requires listening to your own intuition, even if seems illogical?

_____

_____

_____

_____

3. What is your heart's true desire? Do you have an inner knowing of what you need?

_____

_____

_____

_____

_____

FROM A YES TO A NO

It's also normal for your preferences and needs to change, since you evolve and change over time.

As a former people-pleaser, I really challenged myself to move into action and made it my goal to speak my mind more often. I found myself sharing ideas at work and telling more jokes, and it was great for a while! That is, until one day I found myself bickering with internet strangers about their views on race relations. Over time, my pendulum went way too far toward action in a way that wasn't serving me anymore. I was just wasting my time and energy starting useless fights with strangers who just wanted to get a reaction out of me. So my pendulum slowly swung from right to left. I started to practice acceptance that people have different opinions and realized that starting a comment-section war only made both sides more defensive. These days, I am way more at peace by focusing my energy on things that are actually within my control!

JOURNAL PROMPT
Is there any decision that used to be a "yes" in the past, but is slowly becoming a "no"? Why is that?

_____

_____

_____

_____

_____

_____

_____

ATTACHMENT THEORY

We've discussed how important your experience with your parents was, and how it shaped you. But why do children become so affected by this?

Attachment theory has shown that young children need to develop a safe relationship with at least one primary caregiver in order to develop normally. British psychologist John Bowlby first came up with the idea of attachment theory, which proposes that infants' relationships with their caregivers have a great influence on how children later develop and function as adults (Bowlby, 1982).

We all develop an attachment style that's usually based on how we dealt with our parents, and we continue to bring these dynamics into our adult relationships. For example, most of my clients felt anxious and worried about losing love from their parents. Now, as grown women, they continue to choose relationships where they feel anxious and afraid of being abandoned. They can break out of this cycle and develop healthy attachments instead.

Humans are literally wired for connection. I need to emphasize that connection is a *need*. As in, this is not a nice cherry on top, but absolutely necessary for us to grow and thrive. Connection is as important as food, water, and sleep. Babies who aren't touched will fail to thrive, will not develop properly, and can even die. In fact, research from Nationwide Children's Hospital in Ohio has shown that the more you hug children, the more their brains grow (Maitre et al., 2017).

To really drive in the point, I will briefly mention an 85-year study done by Harvard researchers who discovered that the number-one key to a happy, healthy life is positive relationships. Not money, career, exercise, or genetics. Relationships. Let that sink in for a moment.

Just as plants need the right nurturing, environment, and care to thrive, so do you.

Although the full depth of attachment styles is beyond the scope of this book, listen to episode #71 of *The Inner Child Podcast:* WTF Are Anxious & Avoidant Attachment Styles?!

MOTHER AND FATHER WOUNDS

One of my absolute favorite shows growing up was *Arthur*. I especially loved the episodes featuring Arthur's father, who was gentle and silly. I was especially intrigued by a certain Father's Day episode on a video cassette that I borrowed from the library. I obsessively watched and rewatched this episode, carefully observing the interactions between the kids and their different fathers. I didn't know it back then, but my curiosity reflected the longing I had for an emotional connection with my dad.

The best way to explain mother and father wounds is the lack of mothering and fathering. Sometimes your parents might have been physically present, but without a real connection.

Mother and father wounds can usually be summed up with the three A's:

Absence: The physical or emotional absence of a parent. Statistically in the USA, it is more common for fathers to physically abandon families. For example, they may be away for long hours at work and barely be present. Or, they may be a physically present parent but distracted by TV, other family members, or even health issues.

Abuse: A parent who abuses the child. This can include physical, verbal, emotional, financial, sexual, or spiritual abuse.

Addiction: A parent who suffers from alcoholism or drug addiction will naturally experience cycles of being emotionally vacant or volatile and unpredictable. Some addicts are high-functioning and are able to keep up appearances; for example, a mother who only drinks wine the evening.

FIVE WORDS EXERCISE

This exercise can help you determine if you may have a mother or father wound, or both! Write down the first five words that come to mind when you think of your parent. Try not to think too hard or force an answer that sounds more appropriate. Simply allow yourself to write down what naturally comes up for you.

Note: Not everybody is born into a nuclear family with a mother and father! Please use whatever labels and titles are unique to your situation.

FIVE WORDS WHEN I THINK ABOUT MOTHER	FIVE WORDS WHEN I THINK ABOUT FATHER
1. _____	1. _____
2. _____	2. _____
3. _____	3. _____
4. _____	4. _____
5. _____	5. _____

Example: stressed, worries, soft, laughing, serious

Example: serious, silent, "evil eye," newspaper, cold

THE MOTHER WHO ALWAYS WORKED

I had a client named Linh who worked in a design company, who swore up and down that they had a wonderful relationship with their mother. Their mom had immigrated from Vietnam and worked two jobs to create a life for the children. Yet when it came for Linh to complete the Five Words Exercise for their mother, they were surprised that not a single nurturing word came up. The words they wrote were hardworking, busy, religious, cooking, and sacrifice. Tears rolled down their face as I quietly sat with them to process this incongruence. It wasn't that Linh didn't like their mother, as they absolutely loved the woman dearly. But the reality of their experience is that their mother was always occupied with jobs or housework. Linh's inner-child longed to play dolls with their mother and spend quality time together, but they rarely had the chance.

HIDDEN FIGURES

Michelle was a new mother who struggled with feeling codependent in romantic relationships. Memories resurfaced of their father who used to verbally berate them to tears. After doing this exercise, Michelle discovered that they also had a hidden mother wound as well. Their mom, who was always soft-spoken and loving, would instantly disappear from the scene during their father's episodes. Only in the aftermath would the mother reappear and resume their motherly duties. Although their mother didn't participate in the abuse, their silence and complacency allowed for their father's rage to continue for years. This was the first time that Michelle acknowledged and named the hidden anger they felt toward their mother.

What did you discover from these five words? Did it surprise you? Did it reveal anything about your relationship with your caregivers that had been long buried?

PARENT WOUNDS INVENTORY

If the previous Five Words Exercise did not feel deep enough, use the following inventory instead. Read each statement to see if it reflects some aspect of your relationship with your parents as a child, and mark it as true (T), mostly true (M), or false (F). When you're done, review the sentences marked with a T, and circle the sentences that had the greatest impact on you. You are encouraged to highlight these memories in therapy sessions, or make them the focus of a journaling session.

PARENT WOUNDS INVENTORY	T / M / F
1. I often felt alone.	
2. I did not enjoy being around my family.	
3. I did not receive enough hugs, kisses, or loving touch.	
4. I rarely or was never told "I love you."	
5. I was judged or criticized.	
6. I did not receive listening and empathy.	
7. I was only given love when I was "good."	
8. I was abused (verbally, emotionally, sexually, physically) by a parent.	
9. My parent(s) had an addiction.	
10. My parent(s) left or abandoned the family when I was a child.	
11. My parent(s) divorced when I was a child.	
12. My parent(s) died when I was a child.	
13. My parent(s) was in jail when I was a child.	
14. My parent(s) had a serious illness when I was a child.	
15. My parent(s) was overly stressed or anxious.	
16. My parent(s) was depressed or had a mental illness.	
17. My parent(s) paid more love and attention to another child instead of me.	
18. I was rarely or never played with.	
19. I did not respect or admire my parent(s).	
20. I was rejected for who I am (e.g., gender, sexuality, hobby).	
21. I felt pressure to please my parent(s).	
22. My parent(s) rarely or never did activities together (eat meals, watch movies).	
23. I was not celebrated on special occasions (birthdays, graduations).	

GETTING CLOSURE FROM YOUR FAMILY

If your parents are still around and your relationship with them feels salvageable, then you may choose to repair the relationship with them. Doing this is not for everyone and certainly isn't easy, but it may bring you closure and peace at last. If this is what you want to do, try using this template to invite the conversation.

> Dear Father/Mother,
>
> I hope you've been well. Recently I have been doing some soul-searching on my own. I realized that I am carrying some unresolved memories from childhood that are preventing me from moving forward. I know we've never talked about these things before, but it feels like time.
>
> *Optional*: I want to build a wonderful mother-daughter/father-daughter relationship with you, and I hope you feel the same way.
>
> My dream is to meet with you and bring closure to these things that happened, so that we can build a better relationship. Let me know when you're free to meet over coffee.
>
> Your Name

If and when you do meet, my first piece of advice is to seek to reconcile. My second piece of advice is to speak from the heart. There is no template or script that can capture those unspoken words buried inside your heart that only you can find.

Trust your feelings, and don't worry about the words coming out imperfectly! You can only express what is true for you.

If your parents are open to participating in the repair of this relationship, then this is a good sign of hope. This may indicate the start of a brand-new kind of relationship for you! Have patience and allow the budding connection to form naturally over time.

However, sometimes things do not go the way we hope. Parents may reveal to us that they are resistant or defensive, which confirms the reason why you developed this wound in the first place. If that's the case, then it's time to grieve. I know it's painful to be let down in this way, but it takes two to tango in any relationship. You would have done what you could by opening the conversation, and from there, the ball was in their court. Even when the outcome is disappointing, at least you will have a clear answer and not be left wondering.

IS FORGIVENESS NECESSARY TO HEAL?

Every February, my mother calls and asks me to visit and install TurboTax on her computer for tax season. I'll drive over, knock on the familiar painted red door, and be greeted by my smiling mom and the aroma of lunch waiting in the kitchen. We'll chat and reminisce for hours, only scrambling to install the software in the last remaining minutes before I go. I forgot to mention that my mom works on a computer for a living. She could easily do it herself if she wanted to! But after so many painful years of finally healing our mother-daughter relationship, TurboTax became the symbol for our peace oath. It's our own bizarre yearly ritual when we get to connect.

To the question, "Do I need to forgive to heal?" The answer is no.

Forgiveness is a personal choice, and not something you must do out of fear or obligation. Forgiving is also not morally superior to not forgiving, and vice versa.

Some people may have had endured a horrifying experience that perhaps continues to this day, and the choice to withhold forgiveness is empowering. For others, the choice to forgive is more about giving yourself the freedom to let go and move on. There is no right or wrong. What is empowering for you is based on the context of the situation. We all have our personal reasons and the right to do what's best for us. If it helps to hear, forgiveness is also not a permanent decision. You can also make a choice that aligns with you now and change your mind in the future as you evolve as a person.

But if you do choose to forgive your parents and continue a relationship, you will need to be open-minded about what your new relationship will look like. It can no longer be a "parent-child" dynamic where you continue to play the role of the kid. Forgiveness can only happen if you both agree on evolving this into an "adult-adult" relationship where you are on equal footing.

That means you are doing the work equally. You're not secretly waiting for your parent to make a mistake, just so you can point and say, "See?! I *knew* this would happen!" Again, it takes two to tango, and dancing means that the other person will mess up once in a while. There is going to be a "messy middle" period when you are both imperfectly adjusting.

For me, it was accepting that "TurboTax parties" was my mother's love language for quality time. And given that English wasn't my mother's first language, I also had to accept that some things were always going to be lost in translation. That's the beauty, sadness, and complexity of our human experiences!

SIGNS THAT IT'S SAFE TO MEND THE RELATIONSHIP

- You have a personal desire to forgive this person that is not being influenced by societal pressures or urge to please someone.
- You have both shown self-growth.
- You both express interest in mending the relationship.
- You both agree to actively participate in reconnecting.
- You both have realistic expectations about repairing the relationship (i.e., you both understand that it's not going to magically be roses after one conversation).
- You feel open to exploring an adult-adult dynamic with your parent.
- You feel open to forgiving imperfections and mistakes that come up during the repair process.
- You are better equipped to handle your own triggers.
- You are both willing to apologize and take accountability.

FROM CANCER TO COMPASSIONATE

This is a personal story that I shared on my podcast. I had a volatile and, at one point, nonexistent relationship with my father in my adulthood. That is, until he was diagnosed with colon cancer a number of years ago. Faced with the possibility of death, I saw how my cold and cutting father transformed almost overnight into someone I didn't recognize. He became more patient, calm, and thoughtful. He took up acrylic painting, tennis, and even (to our shock!) Zumba dancing. My dad seemed to embrace his own inner-child and chose to live his life colorfully out of nowhere! He was still a bit of that devil's advocate, but it was softer. Luckily, with a surgery and help from his doctors, my father made a full recovery. I believe that his brush with death deeply changed his outlook on life and humbled him. Because of that, I have been open to rebuilding my relationship with him due to our mutual effort to repair things. The reason I share this story is to show that life can still surprise you. With that being said, it's important to still set boundaries and not compromise on empty hopes that someone will change. But in the rare event that someone *does* truly change, will you be open to it? The choice is yours.

QUESTIONS TO GET TO KNOW YOUR PARENT BETTER

Use these questions for inspiration as you are having conversations with your parent or caregiver.

1. What was it like for you growing up as a kid?

2. What are you the most proud of in your life?

3. What did you do with your friends growing up?

4. Did you have any pets as a kid?

5. What was your favorite toy as a child?

_____

_____

_____

_____

6. What do you like about yourself the most?

_____

_____

_____

_____

7. Were you at any big historical events?

_____

_____

_____

_____

8. Who is your hero? Who do you look up to?

_____

_____

_____

_____

9. What's the story behind how you met your significant other?

_____

_____

_____

_____

10. What do you consider the secret to happiness?

_____

_____

_____

_____

11. When you were younger, what did you want to be when you grew up?

_____

_____

_____

_____

12. Can you tell me about the day you were born?

_____

_____

_____

_____

13. If you could change one thing about your life, what would it be?

_____

_____

_____

_____

14. Do you have a favorite song from when you were younger?

_____

_____

_____

_____

15. What are you the most afraid of?

16. How would you friends describe you as a teen?

17. What are the top three most happy moments in your life?

18. If you got a million dollars, what's the first thing you would buy?

19. What do you think is the meaning of life?

20. What's an embarrassing story from your past that feels funny now?

_____

_____

_____

_____

_____

ADDITIONAL RESOURCES FOR REPAIRING RELATIONSHIPS

Parents Are Human Card Game
- Parents Are Human is a bilingual card game that helps you spark deep conversations with your parents and loved ones. (https://parentsarehuman.com)

My Stories Matter
- Preserve your family's stories and legacy in this online app. (https://mystoriesmatter.com)

Storyworth
- Record meaningful moments and memories in a beautiful keepsake book that can then be shared with loved ones. (https://welcome.storyworth.com)

HEALING MOTHER AND FATHER WOUNDS

"One father is more than a hundred schoolmasters."

—George Herbert

For some of you, reconciling with your parents is out of the question. Perhaps this person abused you. Sometimes it's your caregiver who ended the relationship, or died. Whatever the reason, you don't need to justify your decision to anybody. There are still countless ways that we can get you the healing and closure you need.

One thought that has brought comfort to my clients is realizing that the "older adult" role can be filled by somebody other than an actual father or mother. There are so many people who have love to give, so don't be closed off to the idea! Here are creative ways to expand your chosen family and experience relationships that you've never thought of before!

1. GET A DNA TEST TO CONNECT WITH YOUR ANCESTRY

Just because you were dealt a bad hand with your immediate family doesn't mean you have to completely abandon your lineage!

Learning about your ancestors is a powerful way to reclaim your roots in an empowering way. Many cultures around the world believe that our ancestors watch over us from the other side. Perhaps you will find comfort in connecting with a kindred spirit in your lineage. For example, I learned about certain ancestors who were black sheep of the family just like me—painters, musicians, and even one civil rights leader! I pondered about how my own creativity and passion for justice might have been a gift from many generations ago.

It's natural to be curious about where you come from. Obviously, everyone has different opinions and comfort levels with sending out their DNA, but this is an idea one of my students came up with. If you're not comfortable using a DNA service, you can do it the old-fashioned way by creating your own family tree and piecing together details from photo books and interviews with relatives. The cost of using a DNA kit service can range upwards of $100.

Resources:
- 23andMe (DNA testing): https://www.23andme.com
- Ancestry (DNA testing): https://www.ancestry.com
- Family Echo (Creating a free family tree online): https://www.familyecho.com

2. VOLUNTEER AT A SENIOR'S HOME

Offering help at your local senior living facility is a wonderful way to develop healthy friendships with older adults! Not only will you feel good about giving back to the community, you'll also get the chance to create priceless connections with those who may also appreciate the company. Many seniors who have lost their own family are also looking for companionship.

3. JOIN AN INTERGENERATIONAL PROGRAM

Many countries offer various government- or privately run programs designed to build connections between older and younger generations. This can range from living arrangements (where you can live with a senior), to Adopt a Grandparent programs, to even poetry and writing groups where different generations can mingle!

Resources:
- Canada HomeShare program: https://www.canadahomeshare.com
- Generations United (an intergenerational program database): https://www.gu.org/ig-program-database
- Adopt a Grandparent (a virtual program): https://adoptgrandparent.org

4. SEEK NEW ROLE MODELS

I didn't realize this at the start of my own journey, but I used to gravitate toward working with male therapists and coaches who were my father's age. I was unconsciously fulfilling a need to have positive and nurturing male role models in my life. I've also known friends with mother wounds who felt drawn toward working therapists who were older, "motherly" women.

Although some people have disapproving opinions on this, I think it's perfectly valid so long as you're not expecting a professional to replace your parents. Instead, think of it as a safe environment to practice cultivating healthy relationships with someone of that gender. It's also an opportunity to change your narrative and beliefs about men and women!

5. GET ACQUAINTED WITH POSITIVE ROLE MODELS IN MEDIA

There's a reason why certain movies capture our hearts. Even fictional characters provide comfort for the imagination to show us that it's possible for people to have healthy relationships with each other! Which characters do you gravitate toward? Put them on a vision board to help you envision the types of connections you want.

6. CULTIVATE A SPIRITUAL CONNECTION TO MOTHER AND FATHER ENERGY

Thinking of father and mother as universal energies can help those who are spiritually inclined feel free, as it has done for many of my clients. Those who belong to a religion can find comfort in connecting with God or the Heavenly Father. After all, who's to say that love can only come from a human person? You *are* love. Love exists in everything and is around us at all times—you just need to look closely. Is there a natural force in life that makes you feel safe and protected? Here are some examples:

- Connecting to motherly energy when walking through a forest
- Connecting to animals or plants
- Connecting to the spirit of landmarks such as oceans, mountains, rocks, or valleys
- Connecting to rain, snow, wind, or sunshine

- Feeling loved by Mother Earth
- Feeling loved by Santa Claus or Father Time
- Feeling loved by God or the Universe
- Feeling protected by fatherly energy from your favorite tree

CONNECTING SPIRITUALLY

1. Write down how it would *feel* to receive love from mother and father energy. Is it warm? Is it peaceful? What color is it?

_____

_____

_____

_____

_____

2. Visualize being embraced in the symbol you choose for mother or father energy (Example: During a walk in a forest, I imagine being enveloped by the leaves).

_____

_____

_____

_____

3. Allow yourself to receive the loving energy from this experience, giving permission for tears or tender feelings to arise in your body. Write about this experience.

_____

_____

_____

_____

_____

A SPECIAL NOTE TO CHILDREN
OF IMMIGRANTS

I want you to know that I see you. Growing up, I always felt torn between two worlds and two cultures. There was nowhere I belonged fully. It was bad enough that we experienced conflict within the home. I had the added layer of witnessing my parents being targeted for racial discrimination at stores and struggling to speak in broken English. I often stepped up to play the role of a translator and middleman.

I also want to acknowledge that it's normal for your cultural values to sometimes conflict with Western values. For this reason, sometimes I receive criticism when I share that I still have a relationship with my family. These critics who lean toward the side of simply cutting off difficult relationships automatically assume that I have poor boundaries. Why should anyone assume that their values are better than mine?

For example, Asian values like collectivism and filial piety are sometimes seen as enmeshment in the eyes of the Western world that values independence and self-expression. All of us interpret things through our own biases. Neither value is right nor wrong. You can think of values as different-colored lenses through which to look at the world.

Just remember that you're a trailblazer for having a unique identity. You can decide to celebrate not fitting in one box. You don't have to whitewash your identity, but you don't have to completely reject the dominant culture either. You get to pick and choose what values you want to embody. You're allowed to honor the traditions you care about and break the ones that are outdated.

So go on out there and be you!

THE "ISMS"

"Caring for myself is not self-indulgence, it is self-
preservation and that is an act of political warfare."

—Audre Lorde, civil rights activist

I always loved the idea of girl power! I grew up with iconic movies and shows like *Matilda*; *Sabrina, the Teenage Witch*; *Madeline*; and *Xena: Warrior Princess*. And as much as I adored and identified with these characters, there was one small thing that quietly bugged me: none of my icons looked like me!

But when I picked up my first copy of *The Baby-Sitters Club*, I discovered the iconic ponytailed Claudia Kishi. Not only were they an Asian main character (rare at the time), they were a total fashion trendsetter who broke so many stereotypes! This had such a big impact on me.

It feels wrong to talk about childhood trauma without mentioning the complexity of the "isms" (such as sexism, racism, classism, ableism, homophobia, etc.). Forms of oppression like racism aren't about individual comments you might experience from a specific person; it actually refers to how our entire society was originally designed in a way to uplift some people and oppress others. For example, think back to how Black people were treated during the North American slave trade. Even though slavery has technically been abolished, the residual beliefs and practices didn't just disappear overnight. There are still lingering unfair policies and practices that were never changed and continue to affect people negatively today. Some forms of discrimination have mutated into subtleties, also known as "microaggressions." But it doesn't end here in the Western world. Being queer is still illegal in many countries, including the possibility of a death penalty. Women still cannot access education and basic rights in other countries. The list goes on and on, to the point that it weighs heavily on the average person's conscience.

So how can we justify working on our individual inner-child healing when there is a greater world in need? For the big questions like this, I always refer to the idea of putting your own oxygen mask in place before helping someone else. A rising tide lifts all boats, after all. You are in no position to save the world if you yourself are falling apart. In fact, you are continuing to perpetuate the norm of running on fumes and making people concerned about your well-being. I used to avoid dealing with my own issues by trying to help other people instead, and it wasn't coming from an authentic place. So my dear, start with yourself first. Even injured athletes need to take a recovery leave. When you're back on your feet, then you're in better shape to fight the good fight again. My experience is that when more people heal themselves on an individual level, they develop a greater capacity to empower the community around them.

Times are changing, and this is a good thing. We should celebrate the wins while still acknowledging that there's always more work to be done. It is important to acknowledge how the "isms" have shaped you, while at the same time not letting your experiences define your limits and capabilities. You get to define who you want to be!

EXAMINING THE ISMS

What isms have you experienced growing up, and how did that affect you?

1. How did your gender influenced the way you grew up?

_____

_____

_____

_____

_____

2. How has your ethnicity influenced the way you grew up?

_____

_____

_____

_____

3. How has your sexuality influenced the way you grew up?

_____

_____

_____

_____

4. How has your socioeconomic status influenced the way you grew up?

_____

_____

_____

_____

5. How have your body and appearance influenced the way you grew up?

_____

_____

_____

_____

6. How has your health or physical condition influenced the way you grew up?

_____

_____

_____

_____

7. Did I have any diagnoses that influenced the way I grew up?

8. Was there anything "different" about you that influenced the way you grew up?

9. If you experienced multiple isms, how did the intersectionality of your different experiences influence the way you grew up?

10. How do you want to claim and define your identity? How can you truly own the complexity of who you really are? What do you choose to believe or not believe?

HOW TO RE-PARENT YOUR INNER-CHILD (NO, YOU'RE NOT FINE)

Re-parenting yourself simply means finally addressing the needs that you never received as a child. In theory, it sounds simple enough. But in reality, it's hard to recognize your needs when they've been ignored and pushed aside for your whole life!

I really want to convince you of how important your needs are.

At the start of my journey, I tuned out anytime a therapist said I needed to "take care of my needs." What does that even mean?!

Turns out I was never taught to think about my needs as a child because I was conditioned only to think about others. Even the question "What do *I need* right now?" is one that never crossed my mind!

The truth is, I didn't enjoy doing things for myself. It didn't give me that rush of urgency compared to when I was jumping through hoops for somebody else. I only felt motivated to dress up if it was to look good for other people's admiration. I only wanted to cook a nice meal if it meant impressing a man. I certainly didn't just do things *for me only*.

The idea of self-care sounded nice, but my heart didn't fully believe it. That's because I used to routinely go to sleep at 3 o'clock in the morning, skip meals, procrastinate on tasks until the last minute, and chug coffee until my hands were shaking. I believed that my needs couldn't be *that* important if I was still functioning after repeatedly denying them!

What I want to tell you is that those cringey, uncomfortable feelings that accompany doing things just for you will eventually go away, just as with starting any new habit! At first, it feels weird or even wrong. But, over time, it will feel as normal as the air you breathe.

Finally, just because you're used to running on empty doesn't mean you're fine. Merely surviving by the skin of your teeth isn't the same as living a life.

MY SELF-CARE

The first thing to do is examine what underlying beliefs you actually have about needs. This will help you get out of your own way.

1. What does "self-care" mean to you? Try to be as specific as possible.

_____

_____

_____

_____

_____

2. Do you deserve to have your needs met? Are there deeper beliefs that perhaps you don't think deserve to be taken care of? For example, do you feel guilty about putting yourself first?

3. Growing up, what messages were you taught about prioritizing your needs? What messages were you given? For example, were your needs brushed off as unimportant or minimized? Were you taught that it's selfish to take care of yourself, and that other people's needs were more important?

4. What was your caregivers' relationship with self-care? Did your caregivers role-model taking care of their own needs? Did they only help themselves and ignore others' needs? Or, did they frequently deny or sacrifice themselves for the sake of those around them?

5. What's the purpose of taking care of your needs? What do you believe the point of self-care really is?

6. What do you deserve? Do you believe that you deserve happiness and love? Or do you deep down feel that you deserve nothing? Does self-care feel like it needs to be earned? If so, where do you think these beliefs come from?

7. How do you feel about people who prioritize their needs? Do you celebrate seeing others take care of themselves? Or, does it make you feel jealous and resentful? Do you secretly also judge others for being selfish? Remember that judgmental feelings toward others also tend to be things we learned growing up.

8. What beliefs do you need to let go of? Remember that beliefs can be changed over time, just as the belief that a woman's place is only in the kitchen has lost prevalence. Which beliefs are you willing to challenge and let go of? What belief will you put in its place instead?

HOW "HEALED" PEOPLE BEHAVE DIFFERENTLY

The difference between a secure individual and an insecure one, is that a secure person never (or, very rarely) lets the little things slide. Truly taking care of yourself means doing so consistently—not just when you're having a crisis.

A friend named Diana was a role-model for me in this area.

- Diana would take full breaks *all of the time.*
- They prioritized a good sleep over working extra hours *all of the time.*
- They set boundaries at the first sign of an issue *every single time.*
- They taught me that the only person now who's stopping me from living a truly enriched and full life was myself.

This was hard to accept at first. Basing my identity entirely on being a "victim" meant that I could break my own boundaries and find a way to blame someone else for it. But taking responsibility meant being empowered. After all, I'm the one making the choice to speak my truth or not.

HOW TO MEET YOUR NEEDS

"When you're hungry, eat. When you're tired, sleep."

—Lao Tzu

Despite what social media says, self-care is not about expensive spa days and meditating. Self-care is about asking yourself what you need in this moment, and fulfilling it! The best way to illustrate this is using Maslow's hierarchy of needs:

Try this seven-day experiment to become really good at meeting your own needs! Each morning, take a few minutes to answer these 13 questions. You'll find that you will gradually become more attuned to yourself over time!

For the next seven days, take the self-assessment of needs starting on page 108.

SEVEN-DAY CHECKLIST

QUESTION

1. Are you thirsty? Have you had eight glasses of water? Does your mouth feel parched or moist?

2. Are you hungry? Have you eaten your meals today, and on time? Do you feel a stir of hunger inside your abdomen? Have your meals contained proper nutritional value?

3. Are you feeling hot or cold? If you sit still for a few seconds, does your skin feel cool or warm? What is the temperature in the room? Are you sweating and feeling warm, or chilly and cool? Do you need to put on more layers, or take something off?

4. Have you had enough sleep? Do you need to rest? Did you wake up feeling rested this morning? Do you know how many hours of sleep you normally require? Do you feel the urge to take a nap or lie down?

5. What emotions are you feeling? If you sit silently for a few seconds, are any emotions or sensations rising to the surface? If so, where are they coming from? What do these emotions need from you?

6. Do you feel safe in your environment? Do you feel at ease in the room or your current environment? Is your heart rate steady, or do you feel on edge? Do you want to stay, or do you need to remove myself?

7. Do you feel secure in your finances? Do you feel safe and aware of your financial situation today? Are you avoiding looking at your bank account? Are you thinking about money incessantly? What do you need to do in order to get a grasp of your money?

8. Have you met your social needs today? Do you feel connected with others, or are you feeling lonely? If so, what kind of social need do you require? Do you desire an intellectual, comforting, fun, or serious interaction with someone safe?

9. Do you feel safe and comfortable around the people you are surrounded by? If you're around somebody, does your body feel at ease around them? Do you feel like you can openly express yourself? Does your company encourage and bring your best self?

10. Do you feel good about yourself today? How do you actually feel about YOU today? Do you like yourself today? Are you encouraging of yourself today? Do you need to apologize to yourself?

11. Are there two things you can check off your to-do list today that will make you feel more accomplished? For example: Make the bed, pay the bills.

12. Do you feel inspired to do anything creative or fun today? Are you receiving any spontaneous ideas or sparks of creativity that you can channel through writing, drawing, or something similar? Did you feel moved by observing a piece of art?

13. How can you feel fulfilled in your work today? What's one thing you can do at work today that can make you feel accomplished and fulfilled?

DATE RANGE: _____

MON	TUES	WED	THURS	FRI	SAT	SUN

SAY NO TO PERFORMATIVE SELF-CARE!

I once had a client who would only prepare a healthy meal if it meant uploading it to Instagram for everyone to see and praise. Let's not forget to mention the iconic bubble bath selfie that appears to be relaxing to viewers, but instead of resting you're just checking the number of Facebook likes the entire time.

Self-care is meant to be just for you, not for the entertainment and approval of your friends on the internet. Notice if you feel an urge to perform the role as a self-caring person.

TIP FOR PEOPLE-PLEASERS

One of my previous clients was very good at taking care of other people and anticipating their needs, so they told me about how weird it felt to suddenly care about themselves. "But how do I figure out what my needs are?" they asked. The answer was easy! Simply ask *yourself* the questions that you normally ask other people!

If you find yourself constantly asking *other* people how they are feeling, ask yourself! How are *you* feeling today? Where do *you* feel like going to dinner tonight? What movie do *you* feel like watching at the theater?

VISUALIZE ASKING YOUR INNER-CHILD

If you are struggling to come up with answers to these questions, it helps to speak directly to your inner-child. In your mind's eye, picture Little You and ask them directly, "Darling, what do you need in this moment?" Be open to listening to them and responding accordingly. They have been ignored for their whole life, so they may need some patience.

FULFILLING YOUR NEEDS

The most important aspect of re-parenting is giving yourself permission to meet those needs, even if nobody else shares them. No need is too unimportant or insignificant!

You're allowed to pause your Zoom meeting in order to use the bathroom (instead of holding your pee for five more minutes). You're allowed to eat dinner early if you're hungry, even if you're the first person to do it. You're even allowed to be the only person sitting down at the party if you need a break from standing. Even in these examples, you'll see that sometimes our needs may slightly inconvenience other people. I even used to be terrified of telling the waiter that I received the wrong order, out of worry of burdening them.

But as long as you communicate kindly, why is speaking your truth such a terrible thing? After all, you have graciously smiled and accepted *other people's* inconvenient needs all this time! Your sweet inner girl has been ignored and neglected for their entire life, and other people haven't given you *half* the consideration that you give to others. It's time for Little You to be heard and have a seat at the table too.

After being in a healthy relationship with my fiancé for a several years now, I admit that I've become quite a spoiled princess. He wants to take care of me and do the dishes? I say yes. He wants to give me a back massage so I can relax? Yes, please! Attention, love, cuddles, I want 'em all!

HAVE FUN WITH YOUR INNER-CHILD!

At least a few times a year, a client will come to me and say, "Gloria, healing is exhausting. It's depressing, it's heavy, and I'm burnt out."

After a few exchanges, it becomes clear that this person is living an intense healing lifestyle! They suddenly live, breathe, eat, and sleep trauma-healing content 24/7. They're listening to trauma podcasts in the car and scrolling through mental health posts on Facebook in their free time. They're spending long periods of time processing and sitting with painful memories instead of taking a break or leaving the house. It's no wonder they feel totally burnt out!

Girl, if your healing is starting to feel like a burden, then you're doing it wrong! Like all things in life, the heavy lifting needs moments of fun mixed in. Yin with yang. What's the point in doing all this work if you don't allow yourself to enjoy life? Isn't being hard on yourself just another way that you've neglected your inner-child?

I often say to my students that doing the work doesn't come from checking off a list of completed worksheets. It's also not about going to five more therapy sessions than you did last year. Healing is choosing the loving thing for yourself *right now*. And if *right now* your body is tense and wants to move, then in fact dancing to the *Grease* soundtrack is doing the work.

Remember that having fun and letting loose is one of your inner girl's needs too! Personally, I feel more youthful and free now than I used to when I was little. That's because Little Gloria needed to grow up and act adult-like to survive. Now, I give her permission to play, run free, and go wild like the little kid she is!

JOURNAL PROMPTS

1. Write down 10 things that you like to do for fun!

_____

_____

_____

_____

_____

_____

_____

_____

_____

_____

2. Was there anything you liked to do for fun, but adults discouraged or criticized you for it? *For example, parents discouraging your violin-playing because they did not want you to pursue a career as a musician.*

_____

_____

_____

_____

3. What are 10 playful or fun things that you never had the chance to do when you were a child? *For example, Rollerblading, going to a specific museum, making a mess with mud.*

_____

_____

_____

_____

4. Make a commitment to do at least half of the items from your list this year to fulfill your dreams! Write down your plan below. *For example, I commit to booking a pottery class next weekend and signing up for swimming lessons this summer.*

HOW TO BUILD HEALTHY DISCIPLINE

There is a common misconception that self-care is always about resting and sleeping. This is also not true!

There's a reason why my students have made so much progress with the accountability coaching inside my programs. Sometimes, what you actually need is the loving encouragement to *keep going.* The difference is about truly connecting with yourself to find the answer. The Choice Pendulum exercise at the start of this chapter is helpful in these situations too.

Let's use a writing project as an example. If working on this project is literally giving you a headache, depriving you of sleep, and forcing it any longer is going to do more damage, then it's safe to say that rest is needed.

However, if you've only sat with it for 10 minutes and feel tempted to watch Netflix instead, but in your soul you just *know* that there's poetry waiting to be expressed, then perhaps what you actually need is compassionate discipline to inspire yourself to keep going!

The reality is that life *does* present challenges and hard or boring things that must be done! The teeth still need to get brushed. Taxes must be filed. And while loving care doesn't delete the challenges from our lives, it can give us the strength and courage to get through it.

The word "discipline" sometimes gets a bad reputation because it reminds people of toxic hustle culture. However, it's not discipline that's the issue—it's the way that we *learned* how to have discipline. If discipline meant punishment and pain, then your inner-child acquaints it with feeling alone and resentful. But by re-parenting yourself to have a loving approach to discipline, you can turn this into a team sport!

Learn to be a cheerleader to your inner-child instead of a punishing dictator. Try these self-affirmations as a new way to speak to yourself during tough times. And finally, remember that we are hardwired to be social creatures. Ultimately, you need the right environment and community that can hold you to healthy discipline.

10 SELF-AFFIRMATIONS FOR HEALTHY DISCIPLINE

1. "You can do it! I believe in you!"

2. "You have the ability to do difficult and hard things!"

3. "This is the hardest part, but it won't last forever!"

4. "You will feel so proud of yourself when you get through this part!"

5. "It's okay to feel upset or bored. I can feel those emotions *and still do this thing.*"

6. "I can take one step at a time!"

7. "It's okay to make a mistake, I will try again tomorrow!"

8. "I love you, regardless of whether you finish this today or not!"

9. "I'm here for you no matter what!"

10. "I'm the kind of person who can try, try again!"

MEETING ALL OF YOUR PARTS

As you grew up, you were praised for some parts of you and rejected for other parts of you. For example, being obedient and helping others was probably encouraged. Voicing your opinion or being "difficult" was likely discouraged. As a result, the "good girl" part of you has been overdeveloped while the rest of you is underdeveloped. But when you only use *some* parts of yourself, you cannot become whole!

The truth is that nobody is one-dimensional. You are not just a good girl. You're probably also a naughty girl, at times! You're also a strong girl, a funny girl, and a loving girl. You are the whole Universe wrapped up inside one woman. It's time for you to let all of those parts free.

The idea that the human personality is actually made up of a *lot* of parts is not a new idea at all. Freud talked about the id, ego, and superego. The Internal Family Systems model (developed by Richard C. Schwartz) talks about "subpersonalities" within our larger mind. My favorite way of describing it comes from Carl Jung's ideas of archetypes, which is the idea that certain patterns and symbols exist across all cultures and people. These archetypes and "parts" exist within you as well! You are infinite as heck.

For the purposes of this book, let's discuss seven of these "parts" within you! These are the most common parts I work on the most with women.

1. THE INNER CRITIC

The Inner Critic is the part of you who sabotages, hurts, criticizes, and deflects. It feels like a very old mechanism that is fearful and reactive. Sandra noticed that their Inner Critic would flare up anytime they would try to learn something new.

2. THE VICTIM

They are the part of you who feels helpless, powerless, and isolated. The Victim sees the world through a filter of disempowerment and often wants to give up. They blame everyone and everything for their current situation, but at the same time this protects them from taking responsibility.

You might personally know some people who live their whole lives with a Victim complex, deflecting all responsibility to anybody but themselves. For others, it is situationship that brings Victimhood out. For example, my client Jin would immediately shut down and become a Victim anytime they got into an argument with their girlfriend. When you're *in* Victimhood, your mind truly believes that everyone is out to get you! This dynamic created a lot of strain on the relationship when it came to personal accountability.

3. THE PLEASER

They are the part of you who is anxious and worried. The Pleaser is skilled at anticipating other people's emotions. The Pleaser gives and gives, with a hidden expectation that it will return to them someday. They don't set boundaries.

I strongly identified with the Pleaser identity to the point that it even influenced my profession! I believe that I initially chose to become a therapist so that it aligned with my belief that I was a helper. People who are strong Pleasers often walk on eggshells to avoid upsetting others and sacrifice their own needs and well-being for the sake of assisting those around them. This can turn into a cycle of resentment and transactional favors when the Pleaser isn't getting their kindness returned.

4. THE HIGHER SELF/INTUITION

This is the wise, spiritual, ancient, universal, sovereign part of you who knows truth. The Higher Self is the part of you that speaks wisdom in a quiet whisper, even during your darkest moments. Some people experience this as images or just a feeling. Some people from a religious background may associate it with the voice of God.

You might find that even during the hardest days, there is always a tiny voice that knows exactly what you should do. We often ignore this small voice. But the more we listen, the louder and clearer it becomes over time.

5. THE WARRIOR

The Warrior is the Amazonian fighter and a force to be reckoned with. They are your fiercest and most loyal protector who fights for you and pushes you through challenges. The Warrior is the high-achiever, the doer, the risk taker!

I find that women especially struggle with the Warrior, due to social conditioning that women should be soft and gentle. However, women in history have also proven to be powerful, strong, and commanding! Don't be afraid of connecting with this side of you.

6. THE JESTER

The Jester is your naughty, flirtatious, or inappropriate side who doesn't take life too seriously. They are mischievous, indulgent, creative, and wants to run free in the meadow with wild horses!

Unfortunately we've been conditioned to judge ourselves for being bad when we're not in a tidy neat line, not doing what we're supposed to be doing. The Jester says, screw that! We want to break rules, let our hair down, and have some damn *fun*! Nobody feels good to be boxed in as perfect or nice all of the time. You may even feel inspired to dance, make crude or silly jokes, and tease! Shania Twain's hit song "Man, I Feel Like a Woman!" comes to mind as the perfect anthem for the Jester! So let loose and go to town, baby!

7. THE LOVER

The Lover is the passionate side of you who desires to give and receive love, to nurture from a place of abundance. The Lover is your powerful heart center. They feel alive and connected when they are in a safe relationship with a special person. The Lover has so much capacity to hold space for love.

Note that loving is not the same as the one-directional nature of pleasing! It is a balanced effort from both parties involved to create a feeling of being nourished, held, cared for, and carried.

Now that you have a better understanding of all of your parts, it's time for us to connect with where these parts live inside your body. Let's use the Warrior for example: When you think of this side of you, which part of your body do you associate with them? If they had a voice, what would it sound like? What emotions does the Warrior make you feel? What message of wisdom do they bring? And finally, could you give them a name?

Complete this following worksheet to get in touch with all of the parts of you!

EXAMPLE: THE WARRIOR

1. What is their name?

Her name is Wonder Woman, the strong protector.

2. Where do they live in your body?

I feel her like a hot flame in my chest when I need to protect myself.

3. What does their voice sound like?

Her voice is confident, commanding, fearless.

4. What emotions do they make you feel?

She feels like anger (for injustice), adrenaline, power.

5. What messages do they have for you?

She wants me to know that she is going to protect me and move my body into action if I am unsafe.

EXAMPLE: THE PLEASER

1. What is their name?

Their name is Doormat.

2. Where do they live in your body?

I feel them as a rush of anxiety that freezes up in my throat, as if I can't speak.

3. What does their voice sound like?

Doormat's voice is shaky, quiet, like a mouse.

4. What emotions do they make you feel?

They feel like intense anxiety, abandonment, losing love, fear.

5. What messages do they have for you?

This part is a remnant of my inner-child who learned to keep the peace and make others happy in order to stay safe. I can thank them for doing what was necessary at the time to survive. They want me to know that I can also use my empathy skills in healthy situations as well, such as reading a room or connecting with friends.

Try the rest by yourself!

THE INNER CRITIC

1. What is their name? _____

2. Where do they live in your body? _____
_____
_____

3. What does their voice sound like? _____
_____
_____
_____

4. What emotions do they make you feel? _____
_____
_____

5. What messages do they have for you? _____
_____
_____

THE VICTIM

1. What is their name? _____

2. Where do they live in your body? _____
_____
_____

3. What does their voice sound like? _____
_____
_____
_____

4. What emotions do they make you feel? _____
_____
_____

5. What messages do they have for you? _____
_____
_____

THE PLEASER

1. What is their name? _____

2. Where do they live in your body? _____

_____

_____

3. What does their voice sound like? _____

_____

_____

4. What emotions do they make you feel? _____

_____

5. What messages do they have for you? _____

_____

_____

THE HIGHER SELF (INTUITION)

1. What is their name? _____

2. Where do they live in your body? _____

_____

_____

3. What does their voice sound like? _____

_____

_____

4. What emotions do they make you feel? _____

_____

5. What messages do they have for you? _____

_____

_____

THE WARRIOR

1. What is their name? _____

2. Where do they live in your body? _____

_____

_____

3. What does their voice sound like?

_____

_____

_____

4. What emotions do they make you feel? _____

_____

_____

5. What messages do they have for you? _____

_____

_____

THE JESTER

1. What is their name? _____

2. Where do they live in your body? _____

_____

_____

3. What does their voice sound like?

_____

_____

_____

4. What emotions do they make you feel? _____

_____

_____

5. What messages do they have for you? _____

_____

_____

THE LOVER

1. What is their name? ....

2. Where do they live in your body? ....
....
....

3. What does their voice sound like? ....
....
....
....

4. What emotions do they make you feel? ....
....
....

5. What messages do they have for you? ....
....
....
....

LOVING THE PARTS THAT YOU HATE

I know that this exercise can make it incredibly difficult to accept certain parts of us, especially the Victim, the Pleaser, and the Inner Critic. How is it possible to love a part of yourself that has also created so much suffering?!

If you're struggling with this, it helps to see from the perspective of protective mechanisms. As a small child who is completely dependent on adults to live, you had very few options. Pleasing the adults or abuser might have been the only way you could somewhat control the environment. When you still needed to wake up each day and eat breakfast across from the person hurting you, you had to develop certain traits as a child to cope with that. Becoming critical of yourself was a survival instinct in order to stop you from taking risks that might have created further danger. Identifying as a Victim was a way to finally validate that what happened to you wasn't your fault.

Even if you don't love these parts of you yet, you can start with a baby step of at least acknowledging and understanding *why* you had to develop these parts. We can honor that our body will literally do anything it possibly can to defend itself. And trust me when I say that your brain and body will go to great lengths to keep you safe any way. Your body has such deep unconditional love for *you*, that it will literally break itself and develop all sorts of protections in order to protect you.

After all, doesn't your dog instinctively snap at the "beast" to protect itself, even when it turns out that the scary threat was just a vacuum? Even a gentle rose has its thorns to keep itself safe, yet we don't judge flowers even a fraction as harshly as we do ourselves!

Now that you are no longer a small child trapped in that environment, these mechanisms simply are not necessary anymore. Technically you don't need to please people on a daily basis. You also don't need to be so critical of yourself. Finally, identifying too much with being a Victim may have protected you from blame in the past, but it doesn't allow you to take responsibility for your future actions. It is safe to begin letting these parts take a backseat as you step into your new adult life!

With that being said, if you are ever in a real emergency situation, your instincts will kick in and these old parts will spring into action to rescue you!

I have previously used the following car driving example as a visualization tool for how you can utilize all the different parts of you.

Fun fact, I failed my driver's test a couple of times due to being a ball of nerves at the time. When I was preparing to drive alone for the first time, my anxious teacher was nervous about not being there at all. So to compromise, he sat in the passenger's seat next to me to keep a watchful eye of the road. As he gradually became more relaxed, he eventually moved to the backseat. And yes, I did eventually pass and get my license!

Parts sort of work this way too! If an "old" part has been controlling the driver's seat for too long, you can simply invite them to metaphorically shift over to the passenger's seat so that they don't feel completely rejected. We're not trying to "kill" or get rid of parts of ourselves. We're simply expanding our definition of self.

For example, I was ready for my Victim to retire from the steering wheel after disempowering me for so many years. I was able to say to her, "Thank you for doing what was necessary to keep me safe all this time. I'm ready to take the risk and allow Higher Self to drive from now on. We'd still love you to keep watch in the passenger's seat if that makes you more comfortable."

And you'll notice that in the backseat, you have *so* many parts that are alive in your complex and diverse personality! They each get their turn when needed. When you're in a brand-new relationship, your Lover will take the wheel. When somebody is crossing your boundaries, your Warrior can lead the negotiations. When you aren't happy with the painting you drew, you can also invite your Critic to compassionately point out areas of improvement!

Isn't it beautiful how rich and colorful your inner world gets to be? There are no "good" or "bad" parts, they are simply used in different ways.

JOURNAL PROMPTS

1. Which parts do you still struggle to accept?

2. How can you change your relationship with those parts to use them in a more helpful way?

3. Which parts do you appreciate and love?

4. How can you change your relationship with those parts to utilize them more?

5. Which parts are overdeveloped versus underdeveloped?

6. What happens when your Higher Self speaks to the Victim?

7. What happens when the Jester and the Lover work together?

HEALING YOUR INNER CRITIC

"Just give up, you'll never be able to heal."

"Who do you think you are to deserve happiness?"

"You're useless."

Sound familiar? Your Inner Critic might become very loud, even as you navigate this book and work through loving your parts. In my experience, I've found that folks tend to struggle with the particularly difficult Inner Critic.

But what if I told you that your Inner Critic isn't your enemy? What if it's just another part of you to learn how to love?

In our modern-day culture, there seems to be this idea that we're supposed to *fight against* the Inner Critic. I've even heard people talking about destroying it! But if love is about integrating and accepting *all* parts of someone, then what do you think it does to your self-esteem to pick and choose which parts are good and bad?

When I was a ball of anxiety and rage as a teenager, so many adults in my life just labeled me as "problematic." I felt deeply misunderstood and brushed off as being bad. What if your Inner Critic is also being misunderstood… by you?

You see, deep down your Inner Critic is just scared. And as you've pushed them away, your critic became desperate, mean, and loud. Your Inner Critic is akin to a neglected dog at an animal shelter, reactive and snapping out of fear. This part started calling you names to get your attention. The more you ignore and resist them, the more anguished they become in their attempt to get through to you. Why do you think they've been telling you to give up? It's not that the critic wants you to fail, but rather they're worried that you're going to get hurt if you do. It's just fear.

For tips on dealing with intrusive thoughts from your Inner Critic using a single "magic sentence," listen to episode 105 on *The Inner Child Podcast*!

ASKING FOR FORGIVENESS

If your tiny five-year-old niece tripped on the playground, would you say to her, "You're so clumsy. You're garbage. Why would anybody like you?"

This is obviously a loaded question, because there's no way we would ever speak like that to a child we loved! We know that children don't know any better. Children have value just by existing and deserve to be treated well.

Yet you speak to your own Inner-child like this all the time. You may beat yourself down, telling your own five-year old self that they're not good enough. You have likely learned to speak to yourself the same way that you were spoken to. And while what happened to you then isn't your fault, it's still your responsibility to fix things now.

I realized that the reason I cussed myself out so easily was because nobody stopped me from doing it. It seemed like there were no consequences to my actions. After all, it's just me. But the child inside was listening. It finally hit me that I was abusing myself. This realization devastated me! But what I want to let you know is that this exercise isn't to shame you or make you break down in guilt. It's to awaken you to your responsibility to yourself and to see that it's okay to apologize. Healing begins when we own up to our own mistakes.

It's time to apologize to your Inner-child for the way that you've treated them and to mark the beginning of your oath to make things right. Try completing this apology letter template and read it aloud to yourself.

Dear Little _____ ,

I'm sorry for the way that I've _____ .

I made you feel _____ .

I judged, shamed, and criticized you for simply being a child who was protecting themselves. I realize now that you were just _____ .

And although I'm only human and will make mistakes along the way, what I promise to do *differently* than mom/dad/caregiver is _____

_____ .

I will show you my intentions through my actions, no matter how long it takes for us to build trust. I love you.

Love, _____ .

As you read these words out loud, try these tips:

- *Feel* the words inside your body.
- Release the guilt and burden you have carried.
- Visualize a heavy dark cloud leaving your body.

Just as with any other relationship, sometimes one apology isn't enough. Your Inner-child has likely heard many empty promises all their life, and they are waiting to see if you will follow through on your word. Have patience and understanding.

Well done! Over time, you will begin to repair this relationship with yourself and write a new chapter in your life.

TIMELINE EXERCISE

Have you ever discovered an old journal you had and realized you have many recorded memories of things you had forgotten about? That's because our brains will sometimes delete or forget things that happened to us if those memories feel harmful or insignificant.

Creating a chronological timeline of all of your life events can be an empowering tool to take back control of your own story. It helps you organize your memories in a way that makes sense and allows you to notice patterns in your life.

I must caution you that this exercise is not for beginners. It can bring up a *lot* of memories if you're unprepared for it. I recommend doing this at the very end, or with the support of a trusted person. Be patient and gentle with yourself, and give yourself permission to take a break when needed.

For each year of your life, write down all of the significant events and milestones in your life. The chart below ends at age 25, but if you are older, continue the chart in a notebook until you reach your current age. It's okay to estimate the age if you're not exactly sure. You may also refer to journals, photo albums, or other people for more information. For particularly traumatic years, it's normal to have zero or very few memories.

Should I "force" myself to remember things? No, you should never force yourself! The process of documenting your life will feel easier with patience and time. Remember that there's usually a reason why certain memories have been blocked. Give yourself grace.

Is it necessary to remember everything in order to heal? Not at all. In fact, many things happened to you before you even developed the ability to speak. What's most important is being able to identify a pattern of events that have happened to you throughout your whole life.

MY TIMELINE

AGE	SIGNIFICANT EVENT(S)
0	
1	
2	
3	
4	
5	

MY TIMELINE

AGE	SIGNIFICANT EVENT(S)
6	
7	
8	
9	
10	
11	
12	
13	
14	

MY TIMELINE

AGE	SIGNIFICANT EVENT(S)
15	
16	
17	
18	
19	
20	
21	
22	
23	

AGE	SIGNIFICANT EVENT(S)
24	
25	

EXAMPLES OF SIGNIFICANT EVENTS

Transitions

- Changing schools
- Immigrating to a new country
- Caregivers losing jobs
- Moving homes

- Going into foster care
- Divorce or separation in the family
- Significant changes in socioeconomic status

Milestones

- Birthdays
- Graduations
- Holidays or vacations

- "First times" (e.g., First kiss, pet, car, significant toy, passing license, wedding, job, failing something, etc.)

Trauma/Illness

- Abuse (physical, verbal, emotional, sexual, etc.)
- Hospitalization or serious illness/injury
- Death or illness of friends and family
- Death of a pet

- Crime or witness of one
- Accidents
- Addiction in the family or involving close friends
- Breakups, cheating spouses, etc.

Random Vivid Memories

- Memories that you have a vivid or clear recollection of, even if it seems mundane or unimportant

- Arguments and fights within your family or school that you remember vividly

No Memories

- Take note of periods of your life for which you have no memories.

- Repressed memories are a defense mechanism to protect you.

Age 8:

- My pet hamster died unexpectedly, but my mother dismissed my feelings.
- My only friend changed schools halfway through the year.
- First family vacation to Cuba, and it was a happy memory.

TIMELINE REFLECTION QUESTIONS

1. What were your top five most beautiful or wonderful memories?

2. What were your top five most painful memories?

3. Did anything surprise you when you wrote out your timeline?

4. Did you recover memories that you forgot about? What can you do with this information moving forward?

While the timeline can bring back some unpleasant memories, it can also bring back beautiful memories that have been long forgotten.

Here is a Facebook post from a student of my membership, who used this exercise to unlock memories of their inner-child playing at their grandparents' farm. Up until then, their family trauma had overshadowed all of the small pockets of joy that also existed in their childhood.

"Thank you Gloria for connecting me to my inner child. I had buried a playful child for years. Only thing I remembered was being adult or acting like one. I abandoned myself, broke multiple promises with myself. But this week I was able to find happy memories from childhood; they had been buried somewhere. Since yesterday I don't know why I can't stop smiling and finding everything interesting. Feels like just woke up and everything is new and fresh."

Remember that discovering surprising happy memories does not invalidate the difficulties you suffered. It simply means that things don't have to be black and white. The essence of your inner-child is still alive underneath the pain, like a daisy growing through cracks of concrete.

IN SUMMARY

By now, you will have discovered so many things from your past that brought sorrow, joy, and growth into your life. At first, this reawakening may even feel like you are taking steps backwards.

"Why would I open all these painful doors that I shut away and kept hidden all of my life?"

But the buried pain never really stayed completely hidden, did it? We cannot selectively numb emotions, and what happens is we dim all of them, including joy. You've just been coping and living half a life, waiting for the right time to finally feel and process.

This is a great reminder that healing isn't about getting rid of pain, as life includes pain. Healing is about holding ourselves with the pain.

CHAPTER 9

PHASE 3: ATTRACT

"Now go
Occupy spaces
Fill the room
Walk in your crown"
—Malebo Sephodi

First of all, big hugs for coming this far! By this point of the book, you've done the heavy lifting. You've tapped into the power of your emotions and taken back control of the eruptive ones. You've held and healed Little You.

Now it's time to put on your crown, Queen! The Attract pillar is where we save the best for last. This is where things get wild and fun. It's where you get to kick back, sip on your strawberry martini, and reap the rewards of all of your hard work. This is where the magic comes back to life.

Normally, I teach these concepts over many weeks and infuse attraction skills with dating and relationship secrets that call in emotionally available partners. For example, I helped my client Karla call in their first committed relationship after having gone through decades of dating toxic men. It really works! Here, we're going to cover the foundational pieces of attraction so that you can start designing and creating a life you truly desire.

The Attract process is divided into two sections. First, it's all about taking a good honest look at what you're currently accepting in your own life and clearing the crap that is no longer serving you. Once you've created enough space in your life, you can then breathe new energy into it by calling in the things that finally feel aligned with you.

I also know from experience that some of you reading have skimmed through the first two phases and want to get to the good bits now. I get it. You've been carrying around this baggage for so long, and you finally want to feel good. But there's a reason why things need to be done in the right order.

Imagine trying to fly a plane for the first time without learning how to use all the controls first. Or lifting 70-pound weights at the gym without starting with the 10-pound dumbbells first. You're gonna get hurt. Trying to attract new things into your life will epically fail if you haven't done the proper work creating safety with your emotions and addressing your childhood stuff first. People who attempt to cheat and skip ahead end up writing bad reviews saying things like, "It didn't work." Well, it's not going to work if you ignore my suggestions. And, besides, wouldn't it feel worse to then have to start all the way from the beginning again?

If you're feeling impatient and ambitious, that's not a bad thing. That drive is what's kept you alive all of these years. But also know there's no point healing if you don't pace yourself and do it right. Trust the process and the fact that you will get there.

After all, you're a Queen.

WHAT DOES IT MEAN TO "ATTRACT"?

There's a lot of confusing information on the internet about the topic of attraction, which ranges from Law of Attraction, to manifestation, to positive thinking. So what does it really mean to attract something?

For the purposes of this book, I'm going to keep it simple.

Think back to high school when students began to form cliques. You could have a random group of a hundred different teenagers with various hobbies and personalities all within one grade. Yet somehow, the jocks all ended up hanging out with other jocks and got into sports programs. The misfits gravitated toward each other and formed their own group. And oddly enough, the kids who experienced trauma all seemed to buddy up with each other. Why does this happen?

Attraction is simply a two-way process in which you gravitate toward what's familiar to you, and other people infer the same similarities about you based on what you communicate consciously and unconsciously. It's your inner world matching your outer world.

CONSCIOUS COMMUNICATION EXAMPLES

- The words you use
- Your clothing style
- Your outward behavior

UNCONSCIOUS COMMUNICATION EXAMPLES

- Your subtle vocal tonality, volume, confidence
- Subtle body language like how long you hold eye contact, microexpressions, and signs of nervousness, etc.
- Your energy

Confident people appear to magically attract opportunities, but let's take a look at how their body language actually invites this compared to that of an unconfident person:

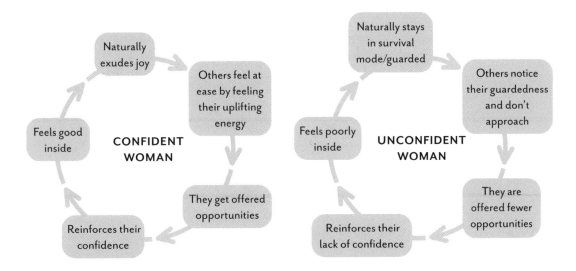

Unfortunately, some experts insist that unconfident women "fake it until they make it." This isn't actually how it works though.

For example, have you ever met someone who was saying and doing all the right things, but for some reason, they came off as sketchy? That's because humans have evolved over a long time to become really good at picking up inauthenticity, even with the most subtle cues.

The best and most sustainable way to attract more good things into your life is to genuinely become more authentic. For example, there's a certain pillar in my teaching curriculum where I coach women how to attract compatible partners without manipulative dating techniques. No silly mind games. No performing and acting to look the part for the sake of impressing someone else. Simply pour your energy into the foundational block of feeling really, really good about yourself and allow the first feedback cycle to kick into gear. You'll be glad you did.

WHAT DO YOU REALLY WANT?

WHAT YOU DESIRE IS WHAT YOU DESERVE

Women have played the supporting role for so much of history. We have been the mothers, wives, caregivers, nurses, and helpers. We are praised for giving to others and criticized for being selfish. But I say, to hell with it! It's time for you to claim what you want.

WANTS ARE FUNDAMENTALLY DIFFERENT FROM NEEDS

While needs are rooted in survival, wants are rooted in abundance.

It's hard enough for women to get their needs met (which we covered in Phase 2), let alone to give themselves permission to experience wants. Yet, we all have them.

When you're daydreaming or fantasizing about the future, what does your heart truly, deeply desire? What does Little You dream of when they're fully connected to their soul?

I knew deep down that I was a romantic and I wanted a partner who would make me feel fulfilled. After healing my own inner-child and breaking out of the dysfunction, I found my partner after just four months! But it all started with the decision that *I deserved what I wanted* and honoring my dreams as something sacred.

GETTING IN TOUCH WITH DESIRE

1. What's the first thing that comes to mind when you think of the word "desire"?

2. When your guard is down, what are the things you fantasize or dream about?

3. What things did your inner girl want when they were little?

---

4. What are your current beliefs about women to honor their wants and desires?

5. Where did those beliefs or biases originate?

6. What did your mother believe about wants and desires?

7. What did your father believe about wants and desires?

8. What does the culture you live in believe about women's wants and desires?

YOUR TYPICAL DREAM DAY

In this visualization exercise, you will begin by visualizing your true desires and wishes. Close your eyes and conjure up an image of what a typical day of your dream life would look like. What's the first thing you see and hear in the morning? What colors are the furniture around you? What does your kitchen smell like? What are you eating for lunch, and where? Whom do you see around you? Hold nothing back and let your imagination run wild! Where are you working? How do you spend your evenings?

Then, write an extremely detailed hour-by-hour itinerary of your dream life starting from the moment you wake up and sign it at the bottom. Allow yourself to flood with excitement as you gush over your day! Keep this itinerary somewhere safe so that you can return to it in the future. You might be surprised at how much ends up coming true!

Now that you've created a vision of your ideal life, we will move onto the two phases that will support you in attracting your desires.

- **Step One:** The Clearing
- **Step Two:** The Calling In

STEP ONE: THE CLEARING

Anytime you sign up for a new class or activity, the first thing you do is remove something else from your schedule in order to make room for it. When you are looking to heal, you also remove yourself from a sick environment.

You can't heal in the same environment that is making you sick.

When I work with clients, we examine multiple areas of their lives that are sucking their energy in ways that they don't even realize. For the purpose of this book, we're going to do a deep dive into just two of these: your home environment and your social environment.

YOUR HOME AUDIT

"Have nothing in your house that you do not know
to be useful, or believe to be beautiful."

—William Morris

There's a reason we call our homes our temple. It is your safe haven. It is the place that you drift off to sleep every night and wake up to each and every morning. And, therefore, your home is an extension of you. It deserves of every bit of care from you.

I truly believe that the way you treat your home is how you treat your life. I have witnessed this truth in family members, in clients, and also in myself. Do you neglect your clothes, letting them pile up and reek for weeks or months on end? If so, what does that say about how much you value your things? Value yourself?

Your things are also an extension of you.

And, by that, I mean that every object and utensil was a decision that you made at one time. These decisions all say something about you.

You might have heard of something called feng shui, which in my culture is an ancient traditional philosophy about arranging your home in a way that creates balance. But you don't need mystical arts in order to create peace in your home! What matters most is that your physical home *matches how you want to feel.*

JOURNAL PROMPTS

1. How do you actually *feel* in your current home?

2. Take a look around at your objects and belongings. What state are your things in? What story does your home tell about you?

3. What do you find beautiful inside of your home?

_____

_____

_____

_____

4. What feels misaligned inside of your home?

_____

_____

_____

_____

5. How would you like to *feel* inside your home, and what needs to change in order to achieve this?

_____

_____

_____

_____

YOUR HOME BLUEPRINT

Take a bird's-eye perspective and draw an ideal blueprint for how you want to arrange your furniture and belongings. What arrangement feels pleasing and balanced to you?

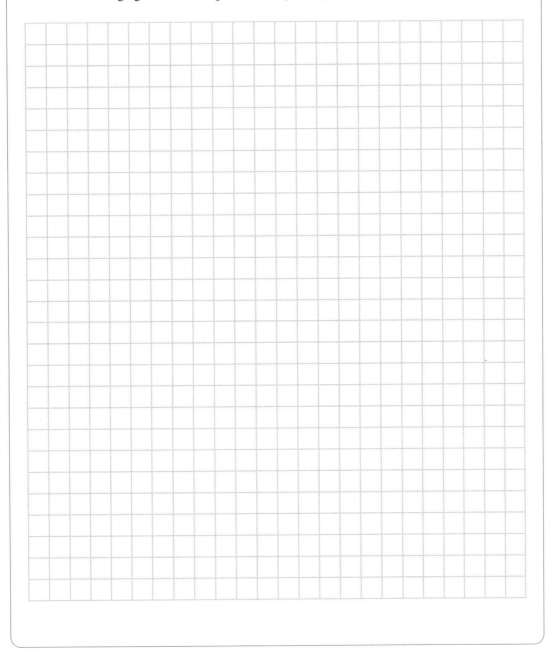

THE SOCIAL CIRCLE AUDIT

"You are the average of the five people you spend the most time with."

—Jim Rohn

The hard truth is that the people you spend the most amount of time with are the ones who influence you the most, whether you're aware of it or not. Have you ever befriended a new gal at work, and then a month later realized you're starting to use the same slang as they do? It's not enough to just purge your Facebook friends every full moon. You need to do a deep-dive analysis to see who's genuinely helping you become the best version of yourself, and who is bringing out the worst in you.

SOCIAL CIRCLE AUDIT

Write down the names of the five people that you interact the most with (in-person or online).

1. _____   4. _____

2. _____   5. _____

3. _____

For each of these five people, answer the following questions:

How do I honestly feel when I spend time with this person?

1. _____

2. _____

3. _____

4. _____

5. _____

What does this person believe about me?

1. _____

2. _____

3. _____

4. _____

5. _____

What does this person believe about themselves?

1. _____

2. _____

3. _____

4. _____

5. _____

What does this person believe about the world?

1. _____

2. _____

3. _____

4. _____

5. _____

How do their beliefs impact me positively/negatively when we spend time together?

1. _____

2. _____

3. _____

4. _____

5. _____

Does this person make me feel safe and help me to grow?

1. _____

2. _____

3. _____

4. _____

5. _____

Example #1:

1. I feel excited and happy when I spend time with Kacey, my best friend.

2. They always tell me that they believe I'm smart, pretty, and deserve the best.

3. Kacey believes that they deserve to work hard and play hard at the same time.

4. Kacey believes that people are mostly well-intentioned.

5. I feel uplifted and hopeful when I spend time with Kacey, and always have a laugh.

6. Yes, I feel safe around them.

Example #2:

1. Although I have fun, I also tend to feel really drained around Ann when they go on routine complaining rants.

2. I'm not sure how Ann feels about me. They smile when we're having fun, but then acts disinterested and unhelpful whenever we talk about anything serious.

3. Ann is always sarcastically self-deprecating.

4. Ann believes that the world sucks and the government is always out to get us, and they are generally paranoid of everything.

5. Although it's nice having company, this relationship stresses me out and reinforces old beliefs that my parents used to have.

This audit is an incredible tool to help you make informed decisions about who is good for you, and who isn't. My client Taj experienced an extremely unhealthy dynamic with their parents, who had criticized them since the moment they were born. It became very clear that merely living under the same roof as them was hindering their growth, and that they needed to get the heck out. I also understood how guilty they felt, as they grew up in a South Asian culture where family ties are important. We equipped them with tools on how to gradually start setting boundaries, and Taj was able to ride off into the sunset and still occasionally see their parents under conditions they felt comfortable with!

PUTTING ALL YOUR EGGS IN ONE BASKET

One common issue I hear about is the question of how to get all your needs met. In terms of friendships, a question I'm often asked is,

"Gloria, should I cut out my fun friends if I can't have deep conversations with them?"

No, not necessarily.

Just as it wouldn't be fair for someone to expect you to fulfill *all* of their millions of needs, we can't expect that of others. It's normal to diversify your portfolio and have different friends for different things.

For example, here's a breakdown of my "baskets":
- Intimacy, touch, and fun needs → My wonderful partner
- Accountability needs → My coach
- Girl talk and reality TV show gossip → My sister

- Entrepreneurship interests → A mastermind community I paid to join
- Anime nerdy interests → An online Discord group
- Party fun needs → A group of girlfriends
- Deep spiritual conversations → My friend Chris

The result? I feel well-supported by all of the people in my life who I have *chosen* to be part of my "tribe." It also means that I don't dump all of my deep spiritual issues onto my colleagues (if they were the only people available to talk to).

Did I also mention that I'm an introvert? Having lots of connections doesn't mean you need to be talking to masses of people all the time, because you have boundaries. For example, I only talk to my therapist a few times a month. I might go out with my party friends only a few times a year. But the few people I spend the most time with are my partner and my sister.

WHAT ARE YOUR SOCIAL NEED "BASKETS"?

What are some "social itches" that you feel the need to scratch? This may include hobbies, lifestyles, or beliefs that you want to have friends to share these topics with. Write your need on top of each of the baskets, using as many as you want.

Examples: Political conversation, gossiping, comedy, knitting, horseback riding, yoga, spiritual, clubbing, pets, salsa dancing, reality TV shows, intimacy

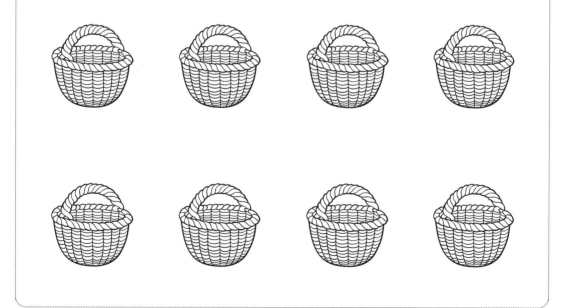

STEP TWO: THE CALLING IN

Now that you've cleared out things in your life that aren't serving you anymore, here comes the fun part: filling it with the things that do!

Remember what we said earlier about attraction being a two-way process, where your inner world matches your outer world?

Look at the desires you wrote down in the Dream Life exercise Step One. These describe your ultimate truth. Are you actually communicating and living your life in alignment with who you are?

WHY AFFIRMATIONS WEREN'T WORKING

It feels like the self-help industry is obsessed with affirmations, but you might have felt like they have been hit or miss! Why is this happening?

Reason: If the affirmation is extremely different from your current beliefs, your mind will reject it as false. For example, my client Sarah felt very insecure about their looks and was going in circles trying to convince themselves "I'm the most beautiful woman in the world."

I began suggesting to my clients to use stepping stone affirmations instead, so that they could work their way up to the new beliefs!

For example:
- "I am in the process of learning to appreciate my looks."
- "I am considering the possibility that I don't have to look a certain way."

Try these templates to come up with your own stepping stones!

STEPPING STONE AFFIRMATIONS
"I am in the process of learning how to…"

"I am opening up to the idea that it's possible to…"

"I am considering the possibility of…"

"I am patiently learning to believe that…"

"I am willing to be open to…"

YOUR VALUES

Values are words that describe what is important to you. Think of them as your internal compass that helps you make decisions.

Write down your list of personal values and circle your top five.

_____   _____   _____   _____

_____   _____   _____   _____

_____   _____   _____   _____

_____   _____   _____   _____

_____   _____   _____   _____

If you need help thinking of words, here is a list of examples to get you started:

Authenticity	Determination	Leadership	Responsibility
Achievement	Doing it differently	Learning	Security
Adventure	Fairness	Love	Self-respect
Autonomy	Faith	Loyalty	Service
Balance	Friendships	Meaningful work	Spirituality
Beauty	Fun	Mindfulness	Stability
Boldness	Growth	Openness	Success
Compassion	Happiness	Optimism	Trustworthiness
Challenge	Honesty	Peace	Uniqueness
Community	Humor	Pleasure	Wealth
Contribution	Justice	Recognition	Wisdom
Creativity	Kindness	Rebel	
Curiosity	Knowledge	Respect	

JOURNAL PROMPTS

1. Do your physical environment and belongings reflect your values?

_____

_____

_____

_____

2. Do your social circle and career reflect your values?

_____

_____

_____

_____

3. If not, what's blocking you from embodying what you really believe?

_____

_____

_____

_____

YOUR ENERGY

Your energy is not any one particular thing about you, but the essence of who you are as a person! It's not about what you wear or what color your hair is. Your energy is you, inside out. It is not what you do, but who you are. Try out these questions to see where your energy isn't in congruence with your values.

JOURNAL PROMPTS

1. How would you describe your "energy"?

_____

_____

_____

2. What color, shape, texture would your energy look like?

_____

_____

_____

3. If your energy had a sound, what would it sound like?

_____

_____

_____

_____

4. How do you want people you like to feel around you?

_____

_____

_____

_____

5. How do you want people you dislike to feel around you?

_____

_____

_____

_____

6. How do other people describe your energy? Does this match how you actually feel on the inside?

_____

_____

_____

_____

7. Do you speak in alignment with your values? Is there anything you want to challenge yourself to do differently?

_____

_____

_____

_____

8. Are you dressing the way that you truly feel on the inside? Is there anything you want to change or find courage to do?

_____

_____

_____

_____

9. Is there anything else in your external world that doesn't "match" your true values and beliefs on the inside?

_____

_____

_____

_____

_____

CALLING IN YOUR ALIGNED ENVIRONMENT

Now that you've examined yourself, it's time to give your home a makeover!

Based on your answers in Your Home Audit (see page 139), what do you need to call into your temple?

1. The vibe I want my home to have is...

_____

2. The colors I want my home to have are...

_____

3. The textures I want in my home are...

_____

4. The plants I want in my home are...

_____

5. The imagery that I want to display in my home's artwork are...

_____

6. The words/quotes I want to display in my home are...

_____

7. I'm more of a minimalist / maximalist. (Circle one)

CALLING IN NEW PEOPLE

Now that you've identified some gaps in your social life from the Social Circle Audit (see page 142), it's time to start filling it up with aligned connections!

First, let's figure out which of your Needs Baskets are missing from your current social life. Did you realize that all of your connections are fun friends, and you're lacking a person to have deep conversations with? Or perhaps everyone around you is pessimistic and serious, and you're in dire need of someone lighthearted and spontaneous? Ask yourself the questions in the following exercise.

FINDING ALIGNED CONNECTIONS

1. What kind of relationship am I longing for? (Examples: friendship, group of friends, romantic, work friend, casual neighbor, etc.)

2. What are the qualities of a connection that I am longing for? (Examples: humor, common interest in brunches, same ethnicity or sexual orientation, friendly)

3. How would I know they have these qualities? (Examples: being part of a group that explicitly states what activity it's for, noticing how you feel in an initial conversation, etc.

---

4. What kind of qualities do these people look for in others?

_____

_____

_____

_____

5. Where would I be able to meet someone like this?

_____

_____

_____

_____

The idea of meeting new friends can feel intimidating to some people, but the truth is that there are so many adults who are desperate to meet new folks! Here are some modern-day ways to find friends:

1. FACEBOOK GROUPS

Facebook has over 10 million Facebook groups filled with people who share interests, from cross-stitching moms to over 40s keto lovers. What's even better is that everyone is there for the same reason: to connect with other people similar to them. You can look for friends who live in your area or who live around the world!

2. MEETUP.COM

Meetup is an international platform and search site where you can find meet-up groups all around the world! Whether it's for learning a language, hiking, or board game nights, you can set the criteria for discovering events, or start one yourself.

3. FRIENDSHIP APPS

Swiping apps aren't just for dating anymore! There are a ton of free and paid apps that allow you to match with compatible friends in your area. Here's a list of suggestions to get you started:

- Bumble BFF: https://bumble.com/bff
- Hey Vina! (For women): www.heyvina.com

- LMK (Audio-based, great for introverts): https://apps.apple.com/us/app/lmk-make-new-friends/id1463320976
- Slowly (For penpals): https://slowly.app/en
- Peanut (For new mothers): www.peanut-app.io
- Friender (For common interests): www.frienderapp.com
- Yubo (For younger crowds): www.yubo.live

CHAPTER 10

CONCLUSION: MAGIC FOR LIFE

"Magic exists. Who can doubt it, when there are rainbows and wildflowers, the music of the wind, and the silence of the stars? Anyone who has loved has been touched by magic. It is such a simple and such an extraordinary part of the lives we live."

—Nora Roberts

Bestie, you did it. Take a big, deep breath in…. exhale. How do you feel?

You've learned the basics of how to take charge of your eruptive emotions and become at peace with your feelings. You know how to reclaim your inner-child's story and re-parent the wounds you picked up from childhood. And finally, you've cleared out the crap in your life and began calling in wonderful things that make you feel fulfilled!

Remember the start of the book when we talked about bringing back the magic? You might have figured this out already, because it's been inside you all along. It's what the meditating gurus have been trying to tell us: every time you fully allow yourself to experience sadness or joy… magic. Not only were you born from the Universe, you are the Universe. Every moment you check in with Little You and ask them how they feel… magic. Every second you decide to let your hair down and dance in the kitchen… magic. Every boundary you set for draining relationships and when you ultimately choose yourself… magic. Every nanosecond you choose to notice the beautiful curve of a loved one's nose, or the faint dewdrop on a leaf… magic.

Magic isn't something we find out there or chase after. It's neither a place, thing, or person. It's an internal choice to see the beauty in anything and everything and can only be experienced inside *your* body. Once we've addressed our traumas and truly held space for our experiences, magic is simply one of those natural by-products of having done the work. It's your natural state of being! It doesn't need to be forced.

And the real beauty is that seeing magic is something that is entirely within your control, no matter what the circumstances are. Nobody can convince you that life is beautiful, ugly, or otherwise. It's a deeply personal and spiritual choice to have the courage to see radiance and charm in the world around us. You can stubbornly choose to have a magical life and see beauty in the pleasure, pain, and everything in between. You can truly see the world through the eyes of a child forever. This is your gift.

This book is only the bare beginning. But even a book can't save your life; you are choosing to save your own life. As they say, healing is a journey and not a destination and is something that evolves throughout your life. These are timeless tools that you can come back to throughout different points of your journey. I didn't hold back and stuffed as many insights and exercises in here as I could! My hope for you is that by healing yourself, you become free of the shackles of your past and live a life of unapologetic joy. And if all of us did the work, we'd leave the world a better place. If you want the free accompanying printables and freebies to this book, grab yours at WomansGuideToInnerChildHealing.com.

I'm proud of you. Heck, I'm *ridiculously* proud of how far you've come.

But, for now, have a beautiful day and an abundant life.

And hold onto that magic.

XOXO

Gloria

BIBLIOGRAPHY

Bowlby, John. *Attachment and Loss, Vol. 1: Attachment*, 2nd ed. New York: Basic Books, 1982.

Bronfman, Elisa T., Elizabeth Parsons, and Karlen Lyons-Ruth. 1992–2008. "Disrupted Maternal Behavior Instrument for Assessment and Classification (AMBIANCE): Manual for Coding Disrupted Affective Communication." 1st ed. Unpublished manuscript, Harvard University Medical School.

Bronfman, Elisa, Sarah Madigan, and Karlen Lyons-Ruth. 2009–2014. "Disrupted Maternal Behavior Instrument for Assessment and Classification (AMBIANCE): Manual for Coding Disrupted Affective Communication." 2nd ed. Unpublished manuscript, Harvard University Medical School.

Lyons-Ruth, Karlen, Elisa Bronfman, and Elizabeth Parsons. "Maternal Frightened, Frightening, or Atypical Behavior and Disorganized Attachment Patterns." *Monographs of the Society for Research in Child Development* 64, no. 3 (1999): 67–96.

Taylor, Jill Bolte. *My Stroke of Insight: A Brain Scientist's Personal Journey*. New York: Viking, 2008.

Porges, Stephen W. "Polyvagal Theory: A Science of Safety." *Frontiers in Integrative Neuroscience* 16 (2022).

Tronick, Edward Z., and Adolph Gianino. "Interactive Mismatch and Repair: Challenges to the Coping Infant." *Zero to Three* 6, no. 3 (1986): 1–6.

Maitre, Nathalie L., Alexandra P. Key, Olena D. Chorna, Pawel J. Matusz, Mark T. Wallace, and Micah M. Murry. "The Dual Nature of Early-Life Experience on Somatosensory Processing in the Human Infant Brain." *Current Biology* 27, no. 7 (2017): 1048–1054.

ACKNOWLEDGMENTS

My loyal podcast listeners, students, and clients have been my biggest source of inspiration behind writing this book. Rock on, besties!

Thank you to my entire team for believing in me and pushing me to cross the finish line with this book. You've made me proud.

And finally, I'm sending love to my darling Andrew for being my rock all this time. He's not just a rock for me, but also for Little Gloria, who finally feels safe.

ABOUT THE AUTHOR

Based out of Canada, Gloria Zhang is a renowned relationship coach, entrepreneur, and former psychotherapist known for her signature style of translating esoteric ideas into everyday wisdom. Gloria hosts the global sensation *The Inner Child Podcast*, a self-help series that has captivated audiences across the globe, accumulating over 1.2 million downloads. Gloria enjoys a quiet life with her life partner, taking pleasure in the simple joys of coffee and anime.